C A S E Y
STONER

Casey Stoner is a two-time MotoGP World Champion – with Ducati in 2007 and with Honda in 2011. Prior to the 2012 French Grand Prix, he announced that he would retire from Grand Prix racing at the conclusion of the 2012 season. In January 2013, Stoner announced that he would move to touring car racing, in the second tier Dunlop V8 Supercar Series for the 2013 season, driving a Triple Eight Race Engineering prepared Holden VE Commodore. He made his V8 debut in February 2013.

www.caseystoner.com.au
@Official_CS27

Matthew Roberts is a sports journalist and television presenter with thirteen years of experience in the MotoGP paddock. Host of the BBC's live coverage of the series, he has also presented coverage of the famous Isle of Man TT race for ITV. A talented writer, he has written on Spanish football for *The Times* and provides regular blogs and features for the BBC website. Matt translated the biography of double MotoGP World Champion Jorge Lorenzo, *My Story So Far*, from Spanish to English and worked with Lorenzo on his second book, *The New King of MotoGP*.

CASEY STONER

WITH MATTHEW ROBERTS

PUSHING THE LIMITS

An Orion paperback

First published in Great Britain in 2013
by Orion
This paperback edition published in 2014
by Orion Books Ltd,
Orion House, 5 Upper St Martin's Lane,
London WC2H 9EA

An Hachette UK company

1 3 5 7 9 10 8 6 4 2

© Casey Stoner with Matthew Roberts 2013

The right of Casey Stoner and Matthew Roberts to be identified as the authors
of this work has been asserted in accordance with
the Copyright, Designs and Patents Act 1988.

Thanks to Andrew Northcott (www.ajrn.com),
Andrew Wheeler (www.autophoto.com) and David Goldman
(www.Goldandgoose.com) for help with photographs.
Cartoon on p.65 by Cheryl Orsini

A CIP catalogue record for this book
is available from the British Library.

ISBN 978-1-4091-2923-3

Printed and bound by CPI Group (UK) Ltd, Corydon, CR0 4YY

The Orion Publishing Group's policy is to use papers that
are natural, renewable and recyclable products and made
from wood grown in sustainable forests. The logging and
manufacturing processes are expected to conform to the
environmental regulations of the country of origin.

www.orionbooks.co.uk

*I would like to dedicate this book to James Strong, AO
(31 July 1944 – 3 March 2013).
James was a massive support to me and my
family throughout my career and I am going to
miss being able to talk to him.*

And to Adriana and Alessandra, always.

FOREWORD

Casey Stoner's story is an incredible journey in both life and racing – from Mike Hatcher's dirt-track in Queensland to MotoGP World Champion conquering the best racetracks in the world. His now famous beaming smile has been seen many times since the first day he raced as a four-year-old, particularly after a successful ride.

But there have been lots of tough times, setbacks, injuries, pain and frustration and disappointments along the way, as with most people who become world champions. Out of the considerable number of people with a lot of ability in any sphere of life, only a select few reach the peak of their sport for reasons more related to the mind and psychology than physical ability. I was lucky enough to get to know Casey and his family through my husband James's and my own love of motor racing and we became good friends. I have seen first-hand the highs and lows of this champion's life. His is a gutsy and inspiring story and I only wish my husband was here to see this finished book. I know he would have loved it!

— Jeanne-Claude Strong

CONTENTS

AUTHOR'S NOTE

'Your time is limited, so don't waste it living someone else's life ... Don't let the noise of others' opinions drown out your own inner voice. And most important, have the courage to follow your heart and intuition.'

STEVE JOBS

Looking back on your own life is a very strange thing, especially for someone pretty young like me. And, to be honest, it is something I've resisted for a long time. Over the years I've had lots of people ask me to tell my story and I have never wanted to; it seemed an odd thing to do because I was so young. It also made me feel uncomfortable, and perhaps a little arrogant, presuming that people would want to know about my life. I like keeping my private life private. Recently, though, my thinking has changed, for a lot of reasons. As I get older I can appreciate that the stories of people who have put in the hard work to follow a dream can inspire others to do the same. That can't be a bad thing.

I've stepped away from MotoGP racing and am now exploring new adventures and challenges. Many people thought I was crazy when I retired at just twenty-seven. However, for me and my family, it has been a long trip with many ups and downs. This is my chance to tell the story of how I achieved my dream of becoming World Champion, and to pay respect to those who helped me or, I should say, us. People sometimes ask me why I refer to myself in the plural sense when I'm interviewed. It's because even though motorbike racing is often seen from the outside as an individual sport, it is actually quite the opposite. No racer can be successful without a good team around them. When I won the MotoGP World Championship with Ducati in 2007 and then with Honda in 2011, I not only had the support of a top team but of an entire factory. I haven't been able to do any of this on my own, it has been a team effort from the beginning, with my parents' support helping us to chase our dream. We wouldn't have been able to reach this goal had it not been for the kindness shown by certain people, people who helped us overcome the obstacles and contend with some of the unfriendly people we encountered along the way. This book is my chance to say thank you and acknowledge the goodwill and encouragement that got me here.

Writing a book is definitely a new challenge for me. I don't consider myself special; I am someone who knows how to ride a bike fast and push the limits of speed. Becoming good at anything takes focus, practice, dedication and persistence and because I was doing something I love, it was easier to stick with it and develop my skills. However, the drive to pick yourself back up when something goes wrong, to 'get back on the bike', is just as important as all those hours learning how to accelerate out of a corner. A combination of all these things, along with the support I received, enabled me to become MotoGP World Champion and has taken me to amazing places and allowed me to meet some astonishing people and create a life I only dreamed of.

Some may say I've been lucky, but I believe you make your own luck. It took an incredible amount of effort to get to this point, a lot of sacrifices and support from my family in the early years and from my wife more recently. I want to acknowledge that support and let people know that if they have a loved one, a child, a partner who is dreaming big, they can go a long way with encouragement.

Family is hugely important to me and recording the experiences I had in the early years of my career for my daughter is another reason I thought the time was right to put pen to paper. I want to tell the real story, not some tabloid concoction. I am not going to sugarcoat anything; I will tell it how it was and is. That is what we do in my family – it seems pointless to do it any other way. Sometimes it may seem harsh or critical to expose some of the bad times. However, I have to be honest about what has happened and the toll it can take to compete at an elite level. This is real life, not a Hollywood movie, and every life has highs and lows no matter who you are.

This is my story. I hope you enjoy the ride. I have. Just for the record, it isn't over yet.

CASEY STONER
2013

PROLOGUE

A *clean, dark strip of tarmac lies ahead, stretching out towards the horizon before seemingly disappearing into the bright blue waters of Bass Strait. Behind me the world's best motorcycle racers sit impatiently on board the fastest two-wheeled machines ever built. Taking a deep breath of that crisp ocean air, I close my eyes and try to think of nothing at all.*

The grid is packed with dignitaries, celebrities and reporters. But behind my sunnies my eyes are firmly closed. There are 53,100 people here to watch from trackside, millions more at home in front of their televisions. There is pressure but, thankfully, pressure is what I thrive on.

It's time.

Turn one, Doohan Corner, at Phillip Island is fast and open. I feel my way through where I can, finding my line as we peel around the long right and then sit up to brake into the long left-hander at turn two.

Turn three is a fast downhill left-hander, almost flat out in fifth gear, and it is probably my favourite corner in the world. It's what I call a 'balls out' corner, the kind of corner that has always seemed to suit me. You get a strong wind coming at you from the inside and it makes you want to lose the front. Some people chicken out when the bike gets light and most riders put weight on the front to carry as much speed as they can. The real key, though, is to get the rear sliding way before you even hit the apex. This takes all the guesswork out of trusting the front through that corner and not knowing whether it will stick or not because of the wind. You have to take the weight off the front and turn with the rear and that's when it really takes guts ...

Twenty-seven laps − the perfect number − I come out of turn twelve for the final time and see the chequered flag being prepared. I am about to win the 2012 Australian MotoGP, my home race. I experience a familiar moment of relief and elation but this time that flag holds extra significance ...

CHAPTER 1

BORN TO RIDE

When they first noticed my ability and my love for bikes, my parents talked about this crazy dream that one day they would watch me stand on the podium as world champion. I was only a toddler when they made a conscious decision to give me every opportunity to achieve that dream, even though others thought it impossible.

My father, Colin, comes from Tamworth, now a major rural city in the New England area of New South Wales, about 420 kilometres north-west of Sydney. It has always been an agricultural hub and farmers in the region produce everything from beef, sheep and poultry to dairy and grain. These days it is well known as an equestrian centre and perhaps best known as the country music capital of Australia.

The fortunes of most Australian country towns are heavily influenced by the weather. The effects of drought and flood can remain for years. Back in the seventies, there was always plenty of work to be had in and around Tamworth for a young bloke keen to make his way. After leaving school my dad tried his hand at pretty much everything: from farming and hunting to property maintenance and training horses. It wasn't out of the ordinary for country blokes to be interested in cars and bikes and Dad was no different. He got into riding bikes when he was fourteen, buying himself an old Suzuki 250 Hustler which he fixed up and rode around Tamworth. After a few years of that he started going to Sydney and Brisbane to race a variety of bikes. It was all pretty basic, though, because he didn't have much money to spare. He'd ride his bike to a meeting, make any repairs or adjustments needed after travelling for hours on the often not-too-smooth highway, tape up the lights so that the glass didn't break all over the track if he crashed and line up with his fellow competitors ready to have a go. Dad liked to race but never had the funds to take it too seriously once he moved to the Gold Coast, which is where he met my mum.

My mum, Bronwyn, had grown up in Southport on Queensland's Gold Coast, part of a family who were heavily involved in horses. She was a real country girl who grew up riding horses from as soon as she was able to sit up. Nowadays when you say 'the Gold Coast' people think

of theme parks and beaches but back in the sixties and
seventies, away from the tourist strip, it was more country
town than glittering city.

A young couple just starting out, my parents made a great
team, doing whatever they could to make a living. They
weren't city people so they wanted to save enough to buy
their own farm, eventually. Mum adapted quickly to a farm
worker's nomadic way of life, and she and Dad would do stints
on different properties, working hard, and hunting foxes in the
winter for the skins. When farm work wasn't so easy to come
by, they'd head back to the Gold Coast and contract as painters
and decorators until they could once again move back to the
country, where they felt more at home.

They got married in 1978 at Werris Creek, a small town
near Tamworth, where they were living at the time. For the
next few years they followed the work, moving back and forth
from the country to the coast, and their first child, my elder
sister, Kelly, was born in 1979 on the Gold Coast. By the time
I was born six years later, on 16 October 1985, my family
were again on the Gold Coast. I was about ten months old
when we went to stay at my grandparents' property for a few
months. While we were living there I had my first experience
on a bike. Like so many other country kids, Kelly had a
Yamaha 50cc PeeWee kids' bike. There was a creek flat just
below my grandparents' house and my dad would take me
out there on the front of the PeeWee. Mum says the first
time I rode the bike my eyes were like saucers. Thinking I

was scared, she told Dad to stop and took me from the bike. Apparently I made it clear I wasn't happy about that, so they put me back on! Mum remembers how my eyes opened wide for a second time. She says, 'I tried to take him off the bike but he hung onto the handlebars. His eyes were like that because he absolutely loved it. After that we couldn't get him off a bike.'

Anyone who knows anything about kids knows how obsessive they can become about things. It can be Pokémon, Lego, ponies or Tonka trucks. My thing was motorbikes, or more specifically that 50cc PeeWee. I was only just walking but I made it very clear that I wanted to ride that bike. Dad was really patient with both Kelly and me and we rode for hours at a time, sometimes joined by my cousin Mark. Dad put in a lot of hours teaching us what to do, so Kelly was already racing bikes at junior meetings by the time she was seven. She became the Queensland Under 9 Motocross Champion, beating all the boys. Being the younger brother, of course I wanted to do what my big sister was doing! Dad would sit me at the front of the bike and teach me about the throttle. He'd say, 'pull it on' as we went up hills and 'let it off' as we went down. I learnt to control the delivery of power from a bike's engine to the wheels at a very young age and by the time I was eighteen months old I'd already suffered the first of many throttle blisters to come.

When I was two we moved back to the Tamworth area, working and living on a family friend's property in a former gold-mining village called Niangala up on the edge of the Northern Tablelands. The land around Niangala is picture perfect: rolling green hills and thick native bush with crystal-clear rivers and creeks winding through them. It is a place of four definite seasons and in winter it can get bitterly cold, enough to snow. Kelly and I thought it was great when it did, mainly because she couldn't get to school.

We lived in the shearers' quarters, a very basic building made of corrugated iron. I didn't care what it was made of, all I needed in life was there. I used to love helping my dad on the property – or at least I'd think I was helping! I guess there isn't a lot of hard yakka a two-year-old could do but Dad would still take me out on the tractor. If I wasn't with Dad on his bike or the tractor I'd be tagging along behind him as he fixed fences or checked the cattle. When he wasn't working we'd go fishing for trout or muck around with Midge, our blue cattle dog, or I'd hang out with Kelly. I really thrived growing up in that environment.

Mum says now: 'He was such a country kid. We went up to the Gold Coast to visit family and it was the first time Casey was aware of being anywhere but the country. We drove past a two-storey office block being built and he said, "Wow, that's a big shearing shed!" He loved living on the property.'

By the time I was three years old my legs were finally long enough for one foot to touch the ground when I was sitting on the PeeWee, which meant Mum and Dad finally let me ride it on my own. I started off just rolling it down to the bottom of the hill near our place and pushing it back up again, rolling down and pushing it back up. After almost wearing a track in the hill, Dad decided I had mastered that enough for him to start the engine up, but not before the video camera came back from the repair shop so that Mum could film my first ride! That set me back by a couple of weeks but I was raring to go as soon as the camera was fixed.

Once I started riding the PeeWee nobody was going to stop me. Kelly had a Suzuki DS 80 by that time and she'd be on that while I rode the PeeWee. We'd ride round and round, having a ball being chased by Midge, until we ran out of fuel. Then we'd hassle Dad to fill the tanks up and we'd go round and round until they were empty again. Eventually it would get dark and we'd have to go inside. It's hard for me to say whether I would have chosen to ride over swinging a cricket bat or kicking a football but living on a property meant most of the time it was only Kelly and me; it wasn't like living in the suburbs where you'd meet up with other kids to play a game of footy or cricket at the park. With my parents' encouragement and nothing else on offer to break my obsession, my love for the bike grew and grew.

It wasn't long before I really got the hang of riding, so I started to look for ways to mix it up. I loved riding after heavy rain because I could spin my wheels in the mud and get into these big fishtails, the back end of the bike weaving from side to side. What better way to amuse a young boy than by making dirt and mud fly everywhere while making heaps of noise? Dad even took the silencer off the bike because I liked the sound. When the ground dried out I'd ask Mum or Dad to pour a bucket of water into a hole to make a muddy patch. I'd put the bike there and hold the throttle and the front brake on so the rear wheel would spin. To me this was all just part of the fun but Dad encouraged my antics because he could see they were teaching me how to be more in control. He was giving me the skills to stay safe. He was also starting to see some potential in me that he wanted to develop, so he told me to try to ride with my feet on the pegs, which was something he knew the famous Belgian motocross racer Roger De Coster did to gain more control. The idea is that if you have your feet up when a motorbike starts sliding around then you have to counterbalance the movements of the bike with your body. Dad could see this was an important technique. Sure enough these movements soon became automatic to me, too, and I quickly learnt how to do a 'donut', where you open up the throttle to spin the rear wheel and turn the bike 360 degrees. My record was eight donuts in a row in long grass, feet on the pegs. I wish I could do that now!

Even when I wasn't riding, I'd be thinking about it. Things would be ticking over in my mind and sometimes that's where the practice was going on. A day, a week or maybe a month after being shown something, I'd be playing around and suddenly it would click into place, even though I wasn't necessarily working on it. I think that happens with any form of practice and it certainly continued for me right to the end of my MotoGP career.

'What do you practise?' Mum used to ask Kelly and me. There was only one correct answer: 'The right way.' Mum applied this to everything we did – riding, chores, school work. It rubbed off on me and even now I don't do anything with the aim of being mediocre. Whether I'm going out to swing a golf club or ski down a mountain I try to practise the right way. There is no such thing as perfect but my approach to anything is a continual quest to improve. There is truth in the saying, 'Anything worth doing is worth doing well.' My mum taught me that.

It's funny, but watching my own daughter grow has opened my eyes more than ever to the incredible extent of children's capacity to learn. People always say that kids learn quickly but in reality I don't think that is totally right. They learn over time through a constant and repetitive process of trial and error. No matter how many times young children are faced with the same obstacle they just tackle it again and again and again, making minor adjustments until they overcome it. Keeping that childhood tenacity is hard but it's worth trying to do so if you can; it can bring huge rewards.

As adults the biggest obstacle we face when learning new skills is fear, and never more so than in a sport such as racing bikes. You can't just keep trying and trying and making mistakes on a bike because mistakes can mean pain and injury. Eventually the threat of pain begins to dictate your limits and

once it has a hold on you there is no breaking through. There
comes a point at any level of motorbike racing where if a rider
keeps getting hurt it is psychologically very difficult for them
to improve any further.

The easiest comparison for me to back up this theory is
with car racing, which I am now learning as an adult. There
is still an element of danger, of course, but the fear of that
danger is limited because you are protected by the stability
of having four wheels on the ground and a cage surrounding
you. As such, the skill of driving a car at speed can be taught
to pretty much anybody over time, assuming they can afford
it because it's an expensive hobby! The best drivers will always
rise to the top, and I'm not taking anything away from them, but
it is a lot easier to arrive at a competent level. You can try new
things in car racing without being afraid of making mistakes
which, in my opinion, is also one of the reasons why the rider
is far more important to the package in bike racing than
the driver is in car racing (the exception to all this is Formula 1
motor racing due to their high speeds and open cockpit).

Young kids are programmed to try things without fear and
by the time I turned four years old in October 1989 I was
developing a broad range of skills on a bike for a child my age.
When Mum and Dad decided to move back to Queensland,
again for work, I was finally able to test those skills against
other kids besides Kelly.

I don't really recall much about leaving the Niangala
property that Christmas but there was something about the

place that had taken hold of me and, as we left, I promised my mum and dad I would come back one day. The feeling of leaving somewhere special was one I was going to have to get used to, because even though I didn't know it as we started the long drive up to Wongawallan in the Gold Coast hinterland, we were covering the first few kilometres of a journey that would not end for another twenty-three years.

CHAPTER 2

HITTING THE DIRT

Our new home at Wongawallan was on the main road from the Gold Coast to Tamborine Mountain. We moved in on New Year's Eve 1989, when I was four years old and Kelly was ten. It was very different from the property at Niangala – the blocks of land were much smaller – but it was still rural enough to keep us happy. Most importantly for a still bike-obsessed child, there was some land around the house which we were able to use as a little track, like the one where I first rode a bike at my grandparents' place. I'd spend hours riding, not knowing I was picking up techniques that would prove useful later in my career. To keep things interesting, Dad used to set up challenges for me, like relays and obstacles to negotiate. The track was surrounded by long grass so if you went off it you'd stall the bike. Dad remembers how he'd try to trick me: 'Casey was so quick I'd cheat by pushing him off his bike into the long grass so that he'd stall the bike and fall over, then I'd hop on his bike and try to steal it. One day when I was making my getaway he launched himself over the front of me, across the handlebars and hit the kill switch. He was four years old, hanging on for dear life! It was all a big game but it showed his quickness of mind; it was all a blur to me.'

I was definitely protective of my bike. I didn't really have other toys or video games or anything like that, I just wanted to ride my bike and I didn't like anybody else touching it. Now we were back on the Gold Coast I was able to get involved in racing and so it was my turn to join the Mike Hatcher Junior Motorcycle Club at Labrador, which was about a 35-minute drive down the highway from our place. Mike Hatcher's was a dirt track and Kelly had already raced there many times before. My first race was on 24 June 1990. Mum removed Kelly's name from an old leather racing jacket she'd outgrown and sewed on a patch that said 'Casey'.

At that very first race Mum started a diary to record how I went and she was diligent at doing so for every single dirt-track race I ever did. In carefully drawn columns she charted the date, circuit, bike, overall position, individual heat position and comments. Those diaries are really interesting to read now, making me remember what those early days were like:

Mum's diary entry, 24/6/1990

Track	Class	Bike	Placings	Overall	Comments
Hatcher's Club Day	Standard	PeeWee	L, 2nd to L, 2nd to L, L, L	L	'Cried before practice but had good fun for the rest of the day & likes racing.'

Mum tells me that the other parents thought she and Dad were awful because I cried as I lined up on the start line. She remembers: 'I was putting his gloves on his hands and pushing his helmet over his head. The thing was, I knew Casey wasn't crying because he didn't want to ride or because he was scared. He just didn't like the attention of being stared at by all those people!'

I am still like that to this day; I genuinely feel uncomfortable about performing in front of big crowds so you can imagine how I felt back then. I had learnt to ride my bike in the peace and quiet of Niangala, alongside Kelly and my cousin. I'd mucked around with some of Dad's mates before this race, but being on a start line, surrounded by other kids and with a whole bunch of people watching, was a very different experience. As soon as that gate dropped, though, I was fine. I was doing what I enjoyed the most – racing – and I didn't care what anybody thought once I was moving.

That first race wasn't about results, it was about learning a new skill on the bike: learning how to race. Over the next few events I improved in every race, eventually picking up fifth place in the last of three races. By August, I took my first podiums, with two wins and three second places out of five to finish second overall in the 50cc PeeWee B-Grade class.

Around this time it turned out I was struggling with chronic asthma. I had the flu and didn't get better for weeks, but there was no way I was going to stay in bed and stop racing. Mum remembers it clearly: 'He was a very sick boy. Our doctor was away at the time and the asthma wasn't picked up by the stand-in doctor. When the paediatrician saw Casey he hit the roof about that. For some reason there are a lot of asthmatics on the Gold Coast but we were told Casey was the paediatrician's second-worst case. You could actually pull his shirt up and see his intestines moving, that's how thin he got at the time. He didn't put on any weight for the twelve months between the ages of four and five. He had glue ear for a while and lost some of his hearing. They tested him for cystic fibrosis and he was on all kinds of medication; you name it, he was on it. But Casey still raced, we couldn't stop him.'

I know I was sick but Mum was right, I wasn't going to let that stop me. In February 1991, at my seventh meeting, I managed to win all five races in the B-Grade category, which meant I had to move up to A-Grade and start all over again. Even though I was still only five years old the class was open to Under 9s, so I was often beaten by the older kids at the club. I also started competing in the 'modified class', which was still for 50cc bikes and Under 9s but having ten-inch wheels and an automatic gearbox were pretty much the only restrictions you had to have.

My 'modified' was a real weapon for a five-year-old, a 60cc Kawasaki that Dad had de-stroked to a 50 by changing the crank shaft to one he had made himself. He pretty much hand-built the whole thing with bits and pieces given to him by an old racing friend of his, Terry Paviell, who had competed with some success over in Europe. That thing used to fly and the 'Kwaka' was my pride and joy.

While we were living at Wongawallan Dad bought himself a road bike and he used to take me out on the back of it to go down to the shops. In the end, though, he had to stop because I would be hanging off the side, trying to get my knee down around the corners like the guys I'd seen on the TV. Dad would have to reach behind and haul me back on.

The bug had definitely bitten, so we started travelling around Queensland to race at different tracks such as North Brisbane, Gladstone, Kilcoy, Trailblazers and Wheelstanders junior bike clubs, racing most weekends with up to fourteen races at each event. Sometimes I'd win them all, sometimes I wouldn't do as well, but I was constantly learning from my successes and failures.

Like many families, we didn't have a lot of money but we got by. Kelly and I knew if we wanted anything extravagant we'd have to save for it and we were soon working out our own ways to make some cash. Living on the tourist road up to Tamborine Mountain gave us the perfect opportunity to make some extra money. On weekends we'd set up a roadside stall, Mum would have made us a bit of guava relish or fruit jam so we could sit out the front of our place with our homemade signs and sell it.

We were racing at Hatcher's every month, then in the winter of 1991, Hatcher's literally became my home track when Dad took up a voluntary position as the circuit caretaker and we moved there, living in a pop-top holiday van borrowed from my uncle until we could afford something bigger. Dad parked it next to the clubhouse on the outside of a bend they called 'Canteen Corner'.

Being able to practise whenever I wanted wasn't the only advantage of living at Hatcher's, it also meant that even when I wasn't on the track riding myself I could watch and learn from the other riders. I remember one night there was a speedway meeting – the first one I'd ever seen – and I was blown away. Watching all these guys come flying around together, totally sideways with the throttle on the stops, I thought, I like the look of this!

Dad remembers the aftermath of that night very well. 'The morning after the speedway we were cleaning up and I put Casey out there to ride, like I normally did, and stood watching as he came up through Canteen Corner for the first time. As he came in he didn't back off, just stuck his leg out and threw the bike in sideways. He looked way out of control. But then he came around and did it again, and again and again, better every lap. I'd been teaching him to ride feet up, wheels in line, which eventually he went back to, but purely through his own observation he now had this extra string to his bow.'

There was one rider I was a real fan of, a dirt-tracker called 'Chook' Cartwright, who would have been fifteen or sixteen at the time. I used to stand pressed up to the wire fence and watch him ride a 250cc; he used to get so low and push the thing so hard, I thought it was fantastic. Then I'd go out and try to copy him. He was a great talent but like a lot of good young riders I guess he didn't have the support to take him to the next stage. It does take a lot of time, money and effort if you want to try to compete at a higher level and for many families it is too hard; there are too many sacrifices to go the distance.

My results at Hatcher's quickly went from podiums in the A-Grade class and wins on the 'modified' to wins in both classes. In August 1991, shortly after we'd moved onto the circuit, I took my first clean sweep of ten wins from ten races; five in each class. For the A-Grade races we'd actually borrowed a PeeWee from a friend. In fact, some parents occasionally used to ask me to ride their kid's bike just to see what the bike was capable of. Mum or Dad would usually have to call me in after a couple of laps though because these bikes weren't used to being ridden so hard and I somehow managed to break a couple of engines. We learnt to be more cautious after that.

After I started winning more times than not, and it was obvious my passion for bikes wasn't wavering, Mum and Dad decided that seeking out sponsors could be a great idea to help offset some of the costs of travelling to meets and keeping the bikes in good order. We were fortunate enough to get the backing of a local Kawasaki dealer, Paul Feeney, who happened to be a long-time friend of Mick Doohan. We had started going into Paul's shop on the Gold Coast to buy parts for the 'modified' and he and Dad hit it off straight away. Paul had a pair of Mick's boots and leathers hanging on the wall of his shop so I would love going in there just to get a close look at them. At the time that shop was probably the coolest place in the world to me.

Paul Feeney explains: 'Colin kept telling me I should come and see his boy ride and I was like, "Yeah, yeah." I'd heard it all before, of course, but I liked Colin, he struck me as a real straight shooter, so I went out to Hatcher's to have a look. Casey was a tiny little thing, timid as, but a really nice kid, always smiling. That's how I knew him, so I wasn't prepared for what I saw that day. He took off and I was just gobsmacked. The thing was on the stops, picture perfect, you couldn't get better. For someone that age, you just don't see that. I turned to Colin and said, "You've got a bit of a talent here, mate," and immediately agreed to help them out.'

Paul started giving us bits and pieces, so you could say he was my first official sponsor. Looking back, he was one of the most important ones because it's hard to imagine that I would have had anywhere near the same level of success I had in Australia without his help. Not only that, he is a top bloke, too.

In October 1991, just before my sixth birthday, I had the opportunity to see two of the masters in action at Hatcher's: Aaron Slight and Scott Doohan. Aaron had won the Australian Superbike Championship that year and Scotty ran second to him, though he didn't go on to have the same success in road racing as his famous elder brother, Mick, who was watching on from the clubhouse that day.

Slighty and Scotty were just playing around but when I was let out onto the track I raced them like I would have raced anybody else. I attacked wherever I could, finding lines up the inside and around the outside that they struggled to take because they were on bigger bikes. A few weeks after that Scott invited me to be a guest at a racing school he was hosting for some Japanese tourists and journalists, who ended up interviewing me for their magazine. It was the first interview I had ever done and Mum still has the clipping from the copy they sent over to us. In return Scott did us a great favour by typing up a letter of recommendation that we could present to potential sponsors.

It read as follows:

To Whom it May Concern,

I first saw Casey Stoner when a few of the local road race boys and myself decided to have a practice on the dirt track at the Gold Coast. We had been riding on the track for a couple of hours and the boys thought they had this dirt track thing pretty well sorted out, then Casey turned up. He was five years old and on a KX 50 so small that the guards were almost sitting on the wheels. Casey then proceeded to show us how to ride the dirt track.

Anyone braking too early on their 250s and 500s and he went straight underneath them and anyone not back on their power early enough had a KX 50 all over them. Since then I have seen Casey ride many times and have come to know his family well.

When instructing at the Pole Position School we had Casey demonstrating to the Japanese how to slide. The Japanese liked him so much that the press members were taking photos of him and doing an interview for Japanese publication.

Casey is a gutsy, aggressive little rider with a huge amount of potential and anyone getting behind Casey and his family would be doing Casey and their own company a big favour.

Yours sincerely,
Scott Doohan

Living at Hatcher's definitely opened up opportunities I might not have experienced otherwise. For Christmas 1991 I was given the best present I could have ever wished for, a fundraiser organised at Hatcher's, with Mick Doohan and Daryl Beattie as special guests, and I was invited to go out and ride the dirt with them as I had done with Scott Doohan and Aaron Slight a few months earlier. Daryl was an ex-Australian flat-track champion and would soon make his name in the 500cc World Championship while Mick, of course, was already a multiple Grand Prix winner and had finished second to Wayne Rainey in the championship that season. This was the man I'd spent countless hours watching on videotape and I was actually going to ride next to him. I was beyond excited.

Paul Feeney says now: 'They put on a display that was probably highly illegal ... pitting the club's young star up against the soon-to-be World Champion in the same race. Casey was riding his little KX 50 and he just gave it to 'em. I mean, Mick and Daryl were messing around a bit but Casey was hanging in there. In the end it got a bit serious because neither of them wanted to get shown up by this kid; he was a bit better than he was supposed to be! But he didn't care who they were, he just wanted to beat them. That was when I said to Colin, "Look mate, if you can keep the whole package together this kid is going to make it. There is no grey area where he's going." Every now and again a kid comes along but he was a level above that. One in a million.'

After watching countless videos of Mick doing battle at circuits all around the world it was unbelievable for me to be out there on the track with him. What we didn't know then was that Mick's career would almost end just a few months later when he crashed at Assen in the Netherlands and the threat of having his leg amputated was very real. I was devastated when it happened because he was easily going to win the championship that year and suddenly it seemed his career was over. The fact that he came back from that injury even stronger and went on to dominate the sport for the next five years was a huge source of inspiration to me, then and now.

Watching people like Mick, Daryl and Kevin Magee helped fuel my passion for bikes. I enjoyed the racing but even more than that I enjoyed the winning and it didn't hurt that on a rare occasion Mum and Dad would give me an ice-cream on the way home to celebrate. Some of the older kids offered me incentives, betting me a Kit Kat or a Freddo Frog that I couldn't win by a certain margin. All these things pushed me to ride harder and faster every time.

I couldn't ride my bike all day, though, as much as I would have liked to. I'd started at a local school, not far up the road from the track, but I hated it from the beginning. It was like being on the start line at that first race, only far worse. There were too many people around for my liking and I didn't settle well into the strict routines of school life. I didn't have much in common with most of the kids because all I wanted to do was get home and ride my bike. Once I was home, I used to stay out and ride until it was dark and I'd be called in for dinner.

Though she liked to do other things, Kelly was still into bikes so we used to challenge each other, riding on one leg, side-saddle or standing on the seat, constantly trying new things purely for our own entertainment. It all helped me learn.

My bikes weren't always the fastest because they were all second-hand, but Dad did his best to get them firing. Quite often we would turn up to a meeting and struggle for the first couple of races but once we got the bike going properly I would usually win. This was pretty much the case when I won my first Australian Short Circuit title over two days in the modified class at Shepparton, Victoria, in December 1991. It was a 1500-kilometre drive to get to the meeting, which shows you the commitment my family had to make to the sport.

After the win, Mum and Dad bought me a cheap bottle of fizzy wine so I could shake it up and spray it all over the bike then pretend to drink from the empty bottle. Like any kid I loved it when I got praise from my parents so those moments of celebration made me fight even harder to be successful in my racing. Going out to win became the only thing that mattered to me. Bikes were everything.

Track	Class	Bike	Placings	Overall	Comments
Australian Short Circuit Titles – Shepparton	*Mod A*	*Kawasaki*	*1, 2, 7, 1, 1*	*1*	*'Didn't like track to start with. Bike wasn't set up for the track on Saturday. Sunday bike & Casey firing & won both races. Last race very close, hard & fast.'*

In early 1992, we were on the move again. We left Hatcher's and after a couple of months living with my grandparents at Paradise Point on the Gold Coast we took some time out at a friend's place in the country and then moved to Coombabah, a suburb not far from my grandparents.

With the moves I didn't race again until the following August, almost nine months from that first Australian title on the Kawasaki. But that didn't mean I wasn't riding, and when I did race I won the Gold Coast Cup with four wins out of four. We then went back to Hatcher's for a club day and I managed to win all five races. I won all five again to retain the Queensland state dirt-track title at Trailblazers in Brisbane, then retained the Australian Short Circuit title at Hatcher's a few days later, even though I had some problems with my bike.

Despite that break from racing at the start of 1992, we'd won twenty-one straight meetings in the modified class between July 1991 and November 1992, including ninety-four wins out of 110 races. I lost my chain in the final race of an event at Wheelstanders club in Oxley, south-west of Brisbane, and ended up third. That broke my winning streak!

When I turned seven in October 1992 I was finally old enough to race geared 50cc and 60cc bikes. Two weeks later at Gunnedah, my second race meeting on geared bikes, I won the Under 9s 60cc class and came second in the 50cc class.

In October 1993 Mum, Dad, Kelly and I packed up again and moved to a place just south of the state border called Deepwater, about 40 kilometres from Glen Innes on the Northern Tablelands. Mum and Dad found accommodation and work on a 1200-hectare property. Just like I had done at Niangala and Wongawallan I made myself a racetrack, riding around and around while imagining big battles with my 500cc heroes.

In between race meetings I'd practise at the home track and I constantly tried to get better, practising the right way. We had figured out that in dirt-track most kids were only using the rear brake to slide into the corners so we tried to gain an advantage by using the front. It wasn't easy because, as anybody who has ridden a motorbike will know, if you lock up the front wheel there is a very good chance you will crash. The trick is learning to find the point where it would lock for a split second, and then releasing it before it would fold.

Dad got a thrill watching how I was developing. He tells of the time we went to a meeting in Canberra: 'There was a long back straight. It was an oil track so it was a hard surface with a big, long straight into a hairpin, and Casey went into it sliding the bike on the front and the rear. He was braking so hard that he turned the tyre on the rim. It was perfect practice for when he started road racing.'

Kids' sport can get ugly sometimes. Left to just the kids I don't think there would be as many problems but when adults get involved things can turn nasty. Sadly, that's what happened to us. Unfortunately all the great results we were getting made me a target. The kids I was competing with were fine but some of the parents started resenting our success. They would complain at every opportunity, suggesting we were cheating and they'd stand at the track going through the rule book to see if there was an infringement of any sort they could pin on me or Dad. My bikes were often taken from me at the end of the races to be checked over. One of the rules was that you had to be strong enough to pick up your own bike and because I was so small a couple of times a few parents would insist that I was stopped on my way back into the pits, and made to lay the bike down to show I could pick it up. On one occasion, after winning a Queensland title race, the officials took the bike off me to scrutinise it and I missed the presentation as a result. I wasn't bothered about picking up the trophy; all I cared about was getting my bike back. They didn't give it back for a week, which was pretty tough on a little kid!

Watching me being hassled and having my abilities questioned and my results tainted, of course got Dad riled up. He is not one to sit back at the best of times and people calling us cheats would never go unchallenged. He was also concerned about the level of safety at some of the meetings and, again, he wasn't going to be silent and let something terrible happen. Sometimes he was too confrontational and more vocal than others and things came to a head in Canberra at the Australian Championship finals in 1993, when Dad complained about the rolling-start system. (Most other dirt-tracks had self-penalising gates, which are the best way to start a race; the gate drops back towards the wheel so if you try to jump the start you get stuck and stall the bike. A rolling start is more dangerous and is usually only used by the seniors, as young kids can get out of control and crash into each other off the start.) He was also concerned there was no flag marshal on some of the corners.

Dad remembers what happened that day: 'Casey was alright, he was winning the meeting. But I wasn't happy with a few safety issues so I went to speak to the officials and was told to piss off. If somebody tells me to piss off I don't take it too well. I told them they were a pack of idiots or perhaps something a little more explicit than that. It was a typical thing, I was just standing up for the kids but I used to get a rush of blood to the head back then and go off pretty hard. They banned me for six months. I appealed it and they gave me twelve!'

By coincidence, Dad also lost his driver's licence for speeding at around the same time he was banned from my race meetings, so Mum had to drive us to every one, there and back, work on the bike, the whole lot. It was tough for her and she didn't get much help from the other parents at the meetings. Sometimes we could push the bike right up against the fence so Dad, who would wait for us outside the pits, could stick his hands through the wire and work on it. Other times we were completely on our own; just me, Kelly and Mum. We certainly found out who our real friends were during this time.

On some weekends off from racing we went to motorcycling gymkhana events organised for country kids not far away in Glen Innes. There would be obstacles set out like a row of poles that you had to weave in and out of, before turning around the end one and coming back through as fast as you could. There was one called 'Cat and Mouse', where two riders would start off at opposite points on a circle and one would have to catch the other. Another event was slow riding, where they'd put a couple of pieces of string out and the person who took the longest time to get from point A to point B would win.

It was a competition but it wasn't highly competitive; it was just for fun, really. Of course, I didn't see it that way, though, and I had dirt and stones flying everywhere. I don't think anyone expected the park to be shredded like it was. When I was on my bike, if I wasn't competing to my maximum level then I wasn't having as much fun.

I enjoyed racing so much that even when I was at home riding on my own I would set up different track configurations to challenge myself. I'd find a rock here, a tree there, a gatepost over there and maybe move a branch and that would be my track. It's something I still do to this day, either with a motocross bike or a dirt buggy. By this time I had also started watching the 500cc World Championship races on television. Like most Australian kids into bikes, I'd ask Mum and Dad to record the races because they were on really late at night, then I'd get up in the morning and watch them over and over. If I wasn't on my bike I was pushing one of those old videotapes into the machine. Other kids get the same way about footy; they can tell you every player in their favourite team and what happened in any particular game. I was exactly the same about bikes. You could ask me about any race, who passed whom in what corner or who won at Mugello in

1988 and why it was so interesting, and I could tell you. I'd watch the champions again and again then I'd go out to my little homemade track and re-create the races on my bike, pretending I was swapping positions with Mick Doohan, Wayne Rainey and Kevin Schwantz. They were all my heroes but Mick was easily my favourite, even before he started winning. There were other Aussies, such as Wayne Gardner and Kevin Magee, but it was always Mick I cheered for the most; there was something about his determination and his never-give-up attitude.

Even though I was still very much in the early stages of my racing career I knew it was what I wanted to do and Mum and Dad were going to back me all the way. They'd already started planning our route to Grand Prix and we'd discussed the possibility of moving to Europe, where the age restrictions were lower, so that I could transfer from dirt-track to road racing as soon as possible. It was already clear that I needed some stiffer competition and after racing a couple of times down in New South Wales, which had been much tougher than in Queensland, we decided that was where we needed to be.

There have been a few successful racers from the Gold Coast, such as Chris Vermeulen, Ant West and, of course, Mick Doohan, but generally speaking the majority of recent Australian talent seems to have come from the Hunter Valley in New South Wales, particularly the areas around Kurri Kurri and Maitland, which are mining towns. I'm not sure why this is but I think it's fair to say these places are tougher to grow up in than the Gold Coast and the area's tradition for hard racing seems to have encouraged some real talent, including the likes of Broc Parkes, Josh Brookes, Jamie and Daniel Stauffer and Chad Reed. Even Troy Bayliss and the Cudlin brothers, Damian and Alex, are from Taree, not too far away from the Hunter Valley region.

All of those guys, apart from Alex Cudlin, were older than me, but there was plenty of talent coming through in my age group, too: kids such as Hayden McBride, Jason Doyle, Daine Stevens and Brad Hellyer, who beat me in my first meeting after we moved to Deepwater.

Brad's father, Lyle Hellyer, recounts what happened at the first race: 'I'd never seen Casey before but one of my mates had told me about him. He'd said, "Hey, your boy is going to be racing Casey Stoner this year." People thought he was going to come and clean up. The first time they raced was at Raymond Terrace, but Colin had been barred from the pits so here's poor Bronny changing the jetting and all sorts of stuff. I can still see Colin up against the fence telling her what to do with Casey's bikes. That was the only time Brad beat Casey seven out of seven. We had Jamie Stauffer's old two-stroke 60cc bikes and they were rockets. I think that got the Stoners thinking, because they'd not been racing anyone fast up in Queensland.'

We'd wanted stiffer competition and we got it in New South Wales; my results proved that. But the fact that I didn't have Dad to work on the bikes took its toll. Mum couldn't match his knowledge. In the early part of 1994 I had a few wins on the 60cc but other than that the highlights were a third place in my first club meeting on an 80cc bike up at Tamworth, and a single win on the 80cc in the B-Grade at Hatcher's. The year ended at the Australian Short Circuit Championship in Albury on the New South Wales–Victorian border in November, where I took the 50cc title but didn't even make the podium in the 60cc and 80cc classes. This was disappointing but also taught me a lot. Mainly that I didn't want to lose!

The solution was already in the pipeline. It had been planned for a while but just over a week after that meeting at Albury we were packing our bags ready to move house again, this time another 500 kilometres further south to Maitland, in the heart of the Hunter Valley. I was looking forward to some regular practice on the circuits down there, ready to do whatever was necessary to get my racing up another gear, and facing other up-and-coming riders regularly on demanding tracks was just what I needed.

Even though things had become difficult with Dad being banned from the pits there was never any question that I would stop racing, and my parents continued to give their full support to me and also to Kelly, who was now cycling at a competitive level herself. It was a juggle but they tried hard not to let either of us down. Once he got his licence back, twice a week Dad would meet Kelly after school and drive her from Maitland to Sydney for her training. It would be past midnight when they got back but Dad would still be up for work early the next morning. On a weekend there might be a cycling event in Sydney so Dad and Kelly would head off again and Mum would drive me to a dirt-track meeting.

Mum and Dad encouraged both Kelly and me to follow our passions and work hard to chase our dreams. That might sound strange when you are talking about a seven-year-old but I don't think you are ever too young to know that if you want something you have to earn it.

There was one saying Dad used to quote that I think sums up my family's attitude to life: 'Aim for the stars and if you hit the moon you're doing pretty well.' It's true, you'll never know how far you can get if you don't have a go!

CHAPTER 3

SAWYERS GULLY SCHOOL FOR MOTORCYCLE RACERS

I was nine years old and already a great part of my life and my family's life was focused on racing. Once we'd moved to Maitland we practised whenever and wherever we could, mainly on the dirt track and speedway over at Kurri Kurri and Raymond Terrace or on the oil track at West Maitland. Oil tracks were basically compressed clay sprayed with second-hand oil and steamrolled so many times over the years that the surface was black and hard, like bitumen. It was slippery, even in the dry, but in the rain it was like ice. You also had to run regulation tyres on the oil, which weren't as aggressive as the knobblies we ran on a dirt track, so the surface stayed more consistent and you could get into long slides without hitting bumps and berms, which made them much more fun to ride.

I had been more used to the dry dust and dirt up at Hatcher's, which was made up mainly of decomposed granite that constantly needed wetting down. It was difficult to maintain the track between races and it would slowly dry out during the day, making it really slippery. You could go out and do three races on a dry surface and then they'd come out and water the track before the next one, turning it pretty much into clay. As it dried again you'd end up with completely different surfaces around different parts of the track, depending on where the sun was shining on it and where it was shaded. I would also be riding different motorbikes in each race so I learnt to be totally adaptable; I had to ride to the conditions and the bike underneath me.

Looking back, I think this is one of the main reasons why Australians with a background in dirt-track gain reputations as 'wet weather riders' in Europe; guys like Ant West and Chris Vermeulen (both fellow Queenslanders) come to mind. Whenever the track conditions are inconsistent you'll see Ant suddenly hit the front, while Chris got his only MotoGP win in the wet at Le Mans and he scored podiums in unusual circumstances, like in the extreme heat at Laguna Seca or at Phillip Island when we had to change tyres midway through the race. Unfortunately, for whatever reason, neither of them were as successful on a consistent basis in 'normal' conditions. Broc Parkes was an absolute legend on the dirt and, once again, fantastic in the rain. Tracks like Hatcher's and similar didn't let you practise on a consistent surface.

Mum and Dad used to stand at the side for hours on end watching me practise at different tracks. They'd sometimes clock laps with a stopwatch as I went round and round. Other parents couldn't see the point in taking it so seriously but they didn't realise it was what I wanted. I was having fun. Working out how I could go faster was how I got my kicks and I couldn't stop until I had taken a tenth or two of a second off my best time on any day. If another kid came out onto the track with me I would be all over them, practising passing them in different ways and in different corners, but most of the time they avoided riding with me and I would be out there on my own, racing the clock.

Dad tells of one particular day at the West Maitland junior dirt-track that really sticks in his memory. 'We were messing about with the bike, setting it up differently and trying different tyre pressures like you would on a practice day at a Grand Prix. The best lap Casey had ever done there was about 20.4 seconds or something similar. This day he managed to get his time down to a 20.1 so I promised him an ice-cream on the way home if he could crack the 20-second barrier before we left. He came past five or six times shaking his head, he knew he hadn't done it and he was right, he was stuck on 20.01. I was amazed he could be so sure of his lap time because he didn't have a timer on his bike. Then he came around on the next lap, crossed the line and nodded his head. I looked down at my stopwatch and, sure enough: 19.98. I could never understand, and I still can't, how he could measure the difference to that degree around a little track like that. It was dirty, slippery, the bike was moving around, there were a lot of factors. And to split a couple of thousandths of a second? That's almost unimaginable.'

When you're riding a track you get a feel for where the speed is coming from and where you are losing time. There might be one corner where you are losing a slight bit of grip and it's not coming together right, so you work at it and work at it until it happens. As soon as it does you know you have found that extra fraction of a second you were looking for. It's all down to a rider having a feeling for the bike and the connection it has with the ground. Eventually you get to the point where you can find this feeling within just a couple of laps. Once you understand where your speed is coming from you can quickly work out where it is lacking and where you can improve. So I would work on that area and keep working on it because I knew I couldn't be faster anywhere else. There is no such thing as perfection but I would concentrate on improving my weaker points, rather than my strong points.

Later on as a MotoGP rider I didn't even bother looking at my lap times because I knew that if the bike was right the lap time would come, so in the free practice sessions, my first priority was always to work on the bike. Once I felt that I could get it to brake where I wanted it to brake, turn in where I wanted it to turn in and get the drive out of the corner that I needed then I knew the lap time would be fast. From there I could make small improvements by introducing little changes to my riding depending on the conditions. Of course, it didn't always work out as planned and we couldn't always get the bike as we'd have liked, but that's racing.

I usually performed my best at major meetings. In 1995 the NSW Long Track Titles were held at West Maitland, where my hours of practice on that track paid off and I managed to win fourteen out of fifteen races and take the overall victory in each of the three categories I entered: Under 13 years 50cc, Under 9 years 60cc and Under 9 years 80cc.

The wins started to come more regularly after that; between April and November 1995 I won more than 200 races (heats and finals included) to take fifty-three overall category wins out of the sixty-five I entered, including four Australian Long Track Titles at North Brisbane and three Australian Dirt Track Titles at Victor Harbor in South Australia.

Mum's diary entry, 28–29/10/95

Track	Class	Placings	Overall	Comments
Australian Dirt Track Championship – Victor Harbor	50cc Open	1, 1, 1, 1, 1, 1, 1	1	Rode very well
	60cc age 9–10	1, 1, 1, 1, 5, 2, 2	1	
	80cc age 9–10	1, 1, 1, 1, 1, 2, 1	1	

We were doing so many miles in the van going to races that we got used to it breaking down. A few times we had to sleep in it on the side of the road; Dad on the front seat, me and Kelly on the rear seat and Mum lying on our tent and blankets across my three bikes, in the back. It never was a great sleep for any of us.

——— —— ——

Maitland was very different from the Gold Coast and a world away from Niangala. Most people in Maitland were great but a few of the local kids were quite messed up, with parents who maybe drank too much, and left them to do what they wanted. These kids formed pretty scary gangs at primary school. I was small and skinny so I was an easy target for them and they'd give me a hard time. School became even less appealing to me because I was being picked on.

The bullying didn't stop once I walked out the school gate. Sometimes they would chase me all the way home. I remember there was a bridge over a river that offered my only escape because I could climb underneath it and squeeze into a narrow gap on top of some pipes, out of their sight. They were too big to follow me so they'd be walking around above me, waiting for me to come out, but I was pretty determined and I'd hang in there until they were gone.

Luckily I had two friends from dirt-track, Sam and Zach, who were twice my size and the sons of a member of a local motorbike club called the Gladiators. The club pretty much owned a whole street so I used to go round to their house quite a bit and hang out. I remember we formed our own club, called the Kiddiators, and I was vice-president for a time. We were only kids messing around but Sam and Zach were monsters at school, bigger than anyone else, and when it became known I was friends with them the bullying stopped. I kind of had 'protection'. School life was a whole lot better after that but I still hated it. All my real friends were from dirt-track; they were the only people I had anything in common with.

There wasn't much free time at the races, not for me anyway, because I was usually riding in three or four different categories so I only got a few short breaks. When I wasn't on the bike my friends and I used to hang out and come up with different things to do. After every meeting we'd find a big enough space and play 'Tackle Bull Rush'. Basically you'd have to try to run from one end of a field to the other without getting tackled by the couple of people trying to block your way. If you were tackled you became a defender as well and had to try to stop others. The winner was the last person to make it 'home' without being tackled.

All the kids at races got on pretty well most of the time and probably would have got along even better if it wasn't for one or another of the parents falling out and then telling their kids who they could and couldn't play with. Some of the kids didn't race fairly, but they were few and far between.

While we were living in Maitland I became good friends with two guys in particular, Brad Hellyer and Jason Doyle, especially after one of the NSW Long Track Title races held in my dad's home town of Tamworth. One of the locals went crazy into the corner off the start and caused mayhem, there were bikes and bodies everywhere. The impact tore ligaments in my shoulder (which would go on to cause me problems later in my career). I was carried off to hospital along with four or five other guys, including Brad, who had broken his ankle, and Jason, who'd wrecked his back.

The next week I got an invitation to Brad's birthday party and his dad, Lyle, will tell you I was already determined I was going to be a champion. Mum and Dad made sure I was eating the right things. 'I remember we gave out meat pies for the kids to eat but Casey said, "I'm not allowed to have these." I told him, "You're at my house now, so you can have some ice-cream as well." It wasn't to spite him or his parents, it's just that's what kids are supposed to eat at birthday parties!'

We weren't used to eating any junk food. For me and Kelly ice-creams and cake were treats, not everyday food. That's what our parents had taught us and they were pretty strict about it. It was ingrained in both of us, especially since Kelly was an elite athlete on the state cycling team and with the Australian Institute of Sport (AIS).

Brad and I liked the same things and that was definitely the start of a strong friendship between us. We used to have fun mucking around at the local speedway or riding our BMX bikes to a local radio-control car track. When I eventually made it into Grand Prix he would often come down to Phillip Island, sneak himself into the paddock without a pass and come and find me in my garage and remind me of the one time he beat me seven out of seven back at Raymond Terrace. Unfortunately, as the years went by, it became more and more difficult for us to stay in touch but it was always good to see him and he never once tried to take advantage of our friendship, which I always appreciated.

———— —— ——

Even at the junior level things can get quite heated during a race. Because I was starting to win a lot, people looked at me differently. It wasn't unusual for other riders to try to find unfair ways to beat me. Some guys would just be loose and out of control but others would deliberately try to stick me in a tyre wall. The classic overtaking manoeuvre in dirt-track is to go around the outside, get into some looser dirt that has a bit more grip and carry that extra speed. Very rarely, if ever, did I go up the inside. So sometimes when I went to go around guys they'd see me coming and try to squeeze me out to the tyre wall. I'm pretty sure that in most cases it was their parents who'd told them what to do but you always had to be careful. I knew who I could trust and who I couldn't and learnt to suss out a rider's body language. You'd get to know when they meant it.

Two of the guys I never had a problem with were Hayden McBride and Daine Stevens. Hayden was becoming one of the toughest competitors I would ever face throughout my career, and though Daine was even smaller than me he was fearless, we often used to go side by side, locked together for a whole lap. While I always felt I had the edge on Daine, Hayden was a totally different story.

Hayden might have had really quick bikes but we never underestimated how good he was either. Although we didn't have the cash the McBrides had, Dad was a good mechanic so it's fair to say that sometimes we had the faster bike, but the racing was still always close. Normally Hayden's bike was better set up from the start, so he could come out of the gate fast. We'd have to spend a couple of races sorting our bike out and then get going. At times my bike would break, so we'd have to borrow somebody else's for a couple of races to keep me in the hunt, then I'd get mine back and it'd be game on again.

This happened one year at the nationals in North Brisbane on the 80cc, when Hayden won the first three races out of a total of seven, meaning I had to win the last four to win the title. He'd come out full of confidence but I'd chase him down and just get quicker and quicker until the momentum turned against him in those national finals. I thrived on the pressure and in the decisive final race I bolted from the gate and took the title.

Dad recalls how this scenario played out a fair bit between the two of us. 'It was always nerve-racking when Casey lost the first three. I'd play around with the bikes and say, "I've done this, I've done that, what do you reckon? You reckon you can do it?" And Casey would just say, "Yeah, we'll be right." I'd say, "Are you sure?" and he'd go, "Yeah, no worries." It was incredible: every time, four in a row. Hayden's father couldn't believe it because they thought they had Casey. It must have driven them mad.'

I liked Hayden, he was a really nice guy. Eventually he gave up racing bikes and went to go-karts instead, which I always thought was a great shame. I heard he went on to become an Australian go-kart champion. I always believed that Hayden would be fast at whatever he did. Under the right circumstances there is nothing he could have achieved that would have surprised me.

Whenever we had a break for a couple of months, like over Christmas, I would be dying to get back racing and I'd come flying out of the blocks. Dad called it giving me 'spells', which is a term they use in horse training, and now and again he used to do it deliberately so I wouldn't get bored with racing, although it was also a good way to ease the financial strain of keeping me racing so often. The start of 1996 was a classic example of that and we won the ACT championship after already taking the NSW Small Track Titles at West Maitland.

Mum's diary entry, 9–10/3/96

Track	Class	Placings	Overall	Comments
Australian Capital Territory State Titles – Canberra	50cc Open	1, 1, 1, 1, 1, 1, 1	1	Rode well on all bikes, well within limits.
	60cc age 10–11	1, 1, 1, 1, DNF, 1, 1	1	Chain came off and locked back wheel in fifth race.
	80cc age 9–10	1, 1, 1, 1, 1, 1, 1	1	

To make more money, Mum and Dad opened a lunch shop in Maitland. This was great for me as my school lunches improved heaps. Between my races, Kelly's interests, trying to earn money and looking after a family there wasn't a lot of time for much more. But Mum and Dad wouldn't let that stop them and always tried to squeeze something else in if they could despite all that. After his bust-up and suspension down in Canberra things had settled down and Dad decided if he wanted to change things in junior racing he'd have to get involved in the decision-making. He became

chairman of the junior commission at Motorcycling Australia,
which didn't pay any money but at least he could have a say
on safety issues. 'It was a lot of work and I constantly had to
deal with people accusing me of making decisions to favour
Casey. I didn't make a single decision based on favouring
him, I didn't have to! The only thing I did was try to get
the minimum age for road racing lowered, but I had a lot
of support for that from various people. I had to deal with
a lot of political nonsense. I remember we had this series
over three different clubs so we made all these trophies,
to try to save money. We sanded them, lacquered them,
sanded them and lacquered them again. They weren't bad
little trophies for the kids and they cost next to nothing, but
we'd bought the lacquer and the timber and stuff ourselves
so we put in a bill for eighty dollars and they refused to pay
it. Motorcycling New South Wales were going to take Lyle
Hellyer to court because he'd signed an invoice on behalf
of the NSW dirt-track committee and they said he "didn't
have the authority". Over an eighty-dollar invoice! This is
why motorcycling is so backward in Australia, the people
who are supposed to be organising it are so petty that it stops
anything moving forward.'

There is no way Dad's involvement in the committee helped
me win races. It had no effect on my results whatsoever.
We managed to win pretty much every title we went in for
that season and after taking four Australian Dirt Track Titles
(Under 13 50cc, 60cc, 80cc and 80cc four-stroke) up at

Hatcher's without too much difficulty, other than the heat, I then had to produce some of the best racing of my career to complete a matching set in the Australian Long Track finals at West Maitland. I won every race on the 50cc and took four out of seven on the 60cc even though I had to borrow a bike because mine blew up in practice.

My only problem was with the 80cc. I was getting bad starts because the gearing wasn't set up right and even though I could get the jump off the line I would get passed quickly because my bike didn't have the drive to get grip. In dirt-track, there are only four lap races on small tracks. In the first final I came from fourth last out of sixteen riders off the line to finish second, and in the second final I came from second last up to third by the end of lap one. A lap or two later I got the lead and bolted. The exact same thing happened in the third final and even though I wasn't able to progress further than second place I took the title comfortably because the two other winners were different so I had the best results overall.

The only disappointing thing about that weekend was the 'Dash for Cash', which they sometimes ran as a bonus race at the end of a weekend. Everybody puts twenty bucks in and the winner takes it all. A whisper went round that I had signed up for the 80cc race so everybody else went in the 60cc race and I lined up against about six guys for only $120; the big money was in the other race! Whatever the prize, I guess I liked the pressure – especially in the Australian Championship. I could be beaten in state finals but once we got to the nationals I barely lost a race.

I mightn't have been riding the shiniest, newest bike but Mum and Dad tried to make up for that. Mum says: 'We would often turn up to race meetings, especially big ones like state titles and Aussie titles, towing our beaten-up little box trailer with three bikes in it and chairs hanging off the side, tyres stacked wherever they could fit. Casey didn't have new bikes, he never had new bikes, but we would give them a little refurbish before an Australian title, maybe he'd get a new lens in his goggles as well, and he used to love turning up like that and then going out there and beating them. He really got a kick out of that.'

The other thing that really fired me up was the other kids sledging around the paddock. It was typical kids' stuff. If I hadn't raced somebody for six months they would say they were going to kick my arse. Most of the time I would try enough just to win but if something like that happened I'd ride as hard as I possibly could to break them. At the risk of sounding too cocky, I was so used to winning that sometimes it would take something like that to motivate me and I'd ride twice as hard.

After I turned eleven we had another three-month 'spell' over the Christmas of 1996, then I came out strong in early 1997, winning 103 out of 104 heats and finals contested between the start of February and the end of April. I was confident and most of the time riding well.

In 1997 I managed to win fifteen state titles in short-track, long-track and dirt-track in New South Wales and Queensland as well as four national dirt-track titles in Canberra before we headed to the long-track nationals at Somersby on the New South Wales central coast to attempt something that had never been done before: five national titles in five different classes (Under 13 years 50cc, age 11–Under 13 years 60cc, age 11–Under 13 years 80cc, Under 16 years 80cc Big Wheel and Under 16 years 80cc four-stroke). You had to be twelve to ride the big wheel so because I was born in October there was just one event that year when I qualified to do all five. It was my chance. There were seven races in each class, some judged on overall results and some split into four heats and three finals.

Mum's diary entry, 8–9/11/97

Track	Class	Placings	Overall	Comments
Australian Long Track Championship – Central Coast	50cc U13	1, 1, 1, 1, 1, 1	1	Rode brilliantly on all bikes. Both...
	60cc age 11–12	5, 1, 1, 1, 1, 1, 1	1	475 fell in first race and took Casey out...
	80cc age 11–12	Heats 1, 1, 1, 1 Finals 1, 1, 1	1	
	80cc Big Wheel U16	2, 1, 1, 1, 1, 1, 2	1	Bike wasn't set up properly in first race.
	80cc four-stroke U16	Heats 1, 1, 1, 1 Finals 1, 1, 1	1	

That was actually my first ever meeting on the big wheel 80, which explains why we didn't have a set-up in that first race, and I got wiped out in turn one of the first 60 race. I had to stop the bike, pick it up and came back to finish fifth. In every other race we were untouchable and to win all five championships was awesome. It still ranks as one of our best achievements because it had never been done before and has never been done since.

Like all my races, Mum remembers it well: 'I think, including practice, Casey rode forty-two times. Because the races were only a couple of minutes long we had to take up this whole U section in the pits. Colin would have the next bike ready to go so Casey could come in, I could grab the bike he had just ridden from underneath him and he'd jump on the other and head straight back to the start line for the next race. This went on for two days! He was actually asked to ride as a passenger in the sidecar that won that day, too, but we decided against it. Despite all that, on our way home Casey wanted us to pull over so he could ride in the bush. That's how much he loved riding.'

I was always like this. As soon as we got back from a race meeting I'd pull the bikes off the trailer and ride them around the yard. I was supposed to be putting them away but I just wanted to ride. Even though I had ridden a lot of races that weekend, as a kid you recover quickly so by the time we finished our trip home I was ready to get back on the bike and start riding again.

W e were a long way from the country, or at least we felt like we were, but we still always liked having animals around us. Sadly our dog Midge had died up at Deepwater, when she caught the disease Parvovirus. We had other pets over the years and in 1998 I had a couple of ferrets, Fez and Zef. I used to take them to the old speedway and send them down rabbit holes trying to chase out rabbits, but Fez was useless. He liked to make himself comfortable down there and fall asleep so I'd have to dig him out.

I was definitely enjoying my racing, but school was proving to be a different matter, especially now that I had moved to high school. My friends had gone to a different school which stuffed me because I no longer had Sam and Zach watching my back. I don't have good memories of my first day there. I didn't know a single person.

We were living at a place called Sawyers Gully, several kilometres from Kurri Kurri near Maitland. Things at high school weren't improving and I was getting increasingly tense and sick. Mum and Dad took me to our doctor, who said it was an absolutely genuine illness, so they decided to home-school me. The education inspector came around a couple of times a year to check my progress. The first time he came he asked me what I'd like to be and I told him: 'Motorbike World Champion!' Since I didn't have any plans to be a brain surgeon, he said to focus on the basic stuff like reading, writing, maths, technology and science. Mum will tell you she couldn't believe the change once I was working one-on-one with her. 'He improved so much and his confidence soared, without the pressure of being bullied every day.' Dad agrees: 'Casey was much happier with Bronwyn teaching him. We used to call it the "Sawyers Gully School for Motorcycle Racers". I was the principal and Bronwyn was the teacher! I helped with science and technology. Among other things, we'd strip down Casey's race bikes and I would teach him about the mechanics. He learnt quickly and was very competent at rebuilding his bikes by the age of thirteen.'

Dad continues: 'Some days Bronwyn and Casey would come to work with me painting. Casey would rub down and paint some of the woodwork for me and I paid him like I would pay anyone else, except the money went into his racing. It was a team effort and I believe that by Casey earning some of the money, it gave him more motivation to succeed. Nothing was handed to him on a platter.'

I don't remember seeing any of the money I earned because it all went back into my racing, although I guess at the time that's all I really cared about anyway. I didn't know anything else. Mum and Dad always said to me: 'If you put in the effort, we'll put in the effort.' It was kind of a mantra and they were true to their word, to the point that they couldn't really say no because I was always putting in the effort. Dad couldn't say, 'I'm sorry, we can't go there this weekend,' because we had a deal. I have carried this attitude throughout my career and I expect everybody around me always to try their hardest because that is what I do. If I give my best then my support team has to as well, and I never give less than one hundred per cent.

We never seemed to be out of work, but things were pretty tight while we were living in Sawyers Gully. Kelly had left school by then and was working as a journalist at the local paper, so she was living her own life. My dad had started budgeting more and more money out of the family income, saving up for the day that we would eventually move to Europe and chase the Grand Prix dream. Dad's theory was that if the money was in the bank he would only end up spending it, so he started withdrawing cash as he earned it and burying it in jars in the yard, where he knew he would not touch it unless he was really desperate. You have to think pretty hard about whether you really want money for something before you dig it up.

Saving money became something of an addiction for him, almost like gambling. The more he saved, the more he wanted to save because he could see the chips building up on the table. If there was a weekend when I wasn't racing he'd work those two days and the money would go straight into a jar. As a family we were living on a very tight budget because we were concentrating entirely on saving.

In July 1998 I won three titles at the Australian Long Track Championship at Albury and three more at the Australian Dirt Track Championship in November, bringing my total to

thirty-five national and fifty state titles. We managed to keep
our form through to the start of 1999, winning an inter-club
meeting at the Central Coast, my first on a 125, with four wins
out of five races. Though I was still very small the bigger bike
seemed to suit me, so now I was just riding the 80cc and the
125cc. I was only entering a couple of classes at each meeting
so we could focus our efforts more.

Since we had achieved everything we set out to achieve
in dirt-track we knew it was time for me to take the next
step and switch my attention from the dirt to the tarmac. We
bought a Moriwaki MH80 road race bike from somebody
at the Australian Junior Road Racing Association with the
intention of entering the Moriwaki 80cc series that summer,
but because I was still only thirteen it was difficult to find
anywhere to practise. In Australia it wasn't actually legal
for any circuit to let me ride until I turned fourteen but we
managed to find a guy at a go-kart track who was willing to let
us do some laps.

After that we also managed to get out at Morgan Park,
Warwick, with Dad's mate Terry Paviell, who had agreed to
help teach me the basics on bitumen. Road racing required
different techniques to sliding around on the dirt and 'Pav' was
very generous with his time. A few years before he'd given me
a pair of Mick Doohan's gloves and boots, which I wore on that
first practice day with Pav on the Moriwaki.

Terry is very modest about his input: 'The Stoners used
to come along to local Queensland road race meetings I was

competing in and Casey was always studying everything very closely. I recall him at around seven years of age, sitting atop a large fence-post by the track at Lakeside for hours. He was learning more than anyone could imagine back then. As I recall the most verbal instruction I gave Casey was on body position and weight distribution, but rather than teaching him new skills I merely translated information he already applied in his riding from the dirt to suit the bitumen, which he did with ease. It was as if he had been pre-programmed to be a road racer, he was extremely quick right from the get-go. He had such a rapid rate of learning it was difficult to structure a program to keep pace, but I knew he didn't need to be lectured in a classroom situation with a whiteboard.'

The main thing Pav taught me was that you can only ride what you can see, which was something that stuck with me throughout my career. I remember a couple of his favourite phrases: 'If you're not sliding you're not riding,' and 'If you're on the grass you're on your arse!' I found out the hard way that the second phrase was true but I actually enjoyed my first crash on the Moriwaki. I lost the front and hit the deck. There were sparks flying everywhere, all this crunching, scraping and noise around me. As it was only a light front crash I got up with no injuries but gained some experience. In later years they would become increasingly painful but that first small crash wasn't bad. I hardly ever used to crash in dirt-track, maybe only once or twice a year, so this was a relatively new thing that I would have to get used to once I started riding road bikes. After that first ride, Pav told my dad I was already riding above the level of the bike and that he would borrow an old Honda RS125 for us to try.

Mum wasn't there the first day I rode the Honda but Dad remembers it well: 'That day the 125cc had very old slick tyres, it was Casey's first time on slicks. He came around a tricky corner and slid off. I went out and picked him up, dusted him off and he got back on the bike. Next lap, he came around even faster and mastered the corner. He didn't crash there again.'

The transition from dirt to road racing took none of my enthusiasm away; I just wanted to get better and better. But I was about to hit a pretty big roadblock. Finally, in October 1999, I turned fourteen and we were able to put in my application for a road racing licence. The application had to be signed by the Australian Junior Road Racing Association (AJRRA), which was essentially a club made up of the parents of older kids I had been racing my whole life. They knew me and knew I was capable of riding a road bike, but they started coming up with excuses for not processing the application. They'd say they hadn't had enough time, or not answer phone calls, things like that. We could only assume it was because they didn't want me racing their kids again and it became really frustrating, to the point that in the end my dad spoke to a mate down in Wollongong who was involved in Motocross. He had all the credentials needed to sign my licence so we decided to do it that way.

Even though I now had my licence I still needed one more piece of paperwork before I could actually race: I had to join the club. It was a stupid rule and, of course, there was only one club, the AJRRA, who clearly weren't too happy about us taking up road racing. It didn't help that Dad had had disagreements with a few of their members from his days as chairman of the junior commission. We had no alternative so we applied to join, sending off our application with a cheque for the joining fee of $50.

While we waited for an official response to my application from the club it seemed to me they were stitching us up any way they could. They did things like organise a practice day then they'd cancel it without telling us, but they'd ring around all the other parents and let them know. On one occasion we drove all the way from Maitland to Sydney for practice and there was nobody there. We just found other places and continued to practise whenever and wherever we could, at different go-kart tracks and on private land.

Terry recalls: 'I just rode as fast as I could and Casey would tag on. It was so much fun charging around, leaning on each other and laughing as we watched the front wheels pattering at high speed. After a few sessions on the MH80 and RS125 I could see Casey getting quicker and smarter with each lap. I ran out of tricks to show him and soon struggled to keep up with the little bugger. His personal characteristics were also extremely strong and apparent; he was a hardened racer who only gave you the opportunity to lean on him once. A touch-up was a great motivator for Casey, whatever I dished up on-track to him would come back on me like a ton of bricks before the completion of the next lap. He just wanted to be the fastest guy on the track and out in front. I was always extremely confident he had more than enough motivation and riding ability to succeed at the top level and I also had confidence in Colin and Bronwyn; dad a great tuner and mum a great motivator and supporter. Together they were a formidable team.'

Finally, after a few months, we got a response from the AJRRA committee. It was a letter addressed to Dad and signed by the secretary of the club. Basically the three lines told us the application had been tabled at a committee meeting and my application to join the AJRRA had been denied.

There was no explanation, no apology, no nothing; just the letter, the cheque and the photo (we still have all three). Effectively I had been banned from racing in my own country at the age of fourteen for absolutely no reason. I was devastated. I didn't care about the politics, whatever they were. I just wanted to race motorbikes and I couldn't understand why I wasn't being allowed to do that when I had the ability. Riding bikes was all I had ever done. It was all I wanted to do. I couldn't understand it; it made no sense. All we could put it down to was jealousy and spite. Even if they had issues with my dad, why take it out on a kid?

We'd been talking about moving to Europe in a couple of years to chase the dream, but only after a year or two road racing in Australia first. Obviously that was no longer going to be an option so the moment we received that letter our plans changed.

Dad says: 'Inevitably, these small-minded people did us the biggest favour. Seeing the sheer anguish they put Casey through was just the motivation we needed to take the plunge and embark on his overseas career.' It was time for Dad to start digging up the backyard!

CHAPTER 4

ANARCHY IN THE UK

It was a huge thing to decide to travel halfway across the world chasing a dream. However, we weren't the first in our family to do it. My dad's parents are both English. They're what they used to call 'Ten Pound Poms', which labelled immigrants who'd arrived in Australia under a scheme set up after the Second World War to increase the population and provide more workers. As part of the lure, the Australian government helped with the cost of travelling so that Brits (and others from Commonwealth countries) only had to pay ten pounds sterling to make the trip and their kids travelled for free, as long as they didn't return within two years. After the bleakness of the war years in England, a chance to make a better life sounded good.

Pop knew a bit about Australia already. He'd been stationed in Hong Kong during the war and made friends with a bunch of Aussie guys who told him plenty of stories about what life was like 'Down Under', and he liked what he heard. In 1949, four years after the war ended, he and Nan took the plunge and jumped on a boat. My Uncle Peter was born the following year, Uncle Ron four years later and my father, Colin, two years after that. Australia was a cheap country for day-to-day living in the fifties and if you wanted to work extra hours then there was plenty of opportunity to do so. Pop set up in the building trade and did well for himself, far better than he ever could have back in England. He wasn't afraid of hard work, and he passed his work ethic on to my dad, who has passed it on to me. It was drilled into me from a very young age that life is what you are prepared to make of it and, even to this day, the opportunities are endless in Australia. Endless, maybe, until you decide you want to be a professional motorcycle racer!

The disappointment in receiving that rejected application to join the AJRRA soon turned to anger and then to a steely determination not to let it beat us. I had a drawing on my bedroom wall, next to all the motorcycle posters, of a frog inside the mouth of a pelican. All you could see of the frog was part of its body and its legs hanging out of the beak. Its front legs were wrapped around the throat of the pelican, choking it and making sure the bird couldn't swallow. The caption said: NEVER EVER GIVE UP. I believed, and my parents believed, that I had what it took to compete at an elite level if I

Never ever give up!

had the chance. No one was going to make that happen except us, so just one generation on from my grandparents taking that boat from Southampton to Sydney, Mum, Dad and I found ourselves making the return trip thanks to Dad being able to obtain British passports. Thankfully the days of having to spend six weeks at sea were long gone and on 25 January 2000, we boarded a flight from Sydney to London via Kuala Lumpur and Abu Dhabi. I'd never been on an aeroplane before that. Kelly stayed in Australia, she was almost twenty-one and had spent a great deal of her teen years travelling around with us while I competed. It was hard for her to watch us go and I know she struggled with the decision a little. I understand that, we were travelling to the other side of the world.

Having left Sydney in the middle of summer, we landed in London to a temperature of minus three degrees, which was definitely a shock to the system. We made our way from the luggage carousel to our hire car and loaded our cases, stuffed with just our clothes, a set of white Harley-Davidson leathers

Terry Pav had given me and some light tools for Dad. Our first stop was Worthing on the south coast to spend a few nights with Dad's Uncle Frank and Auntie Mary. While we were there we bought an old yellow LDV van and a caravan, which would be our home.

Next stop was Southport, a small town on the north-west coast of England between Liverpool and Blackpool. Dad had arranged to meet a guy there by the name of Ian Newton, whose number he'd found through a link on a website promoting the Aprilia Cup motorcycle youth series in Italy. Aprilia is an Italian motorcycle company. Ian was running a similar championship in the UK, the Aprilia Superteen Challenge for 12–18-year-olds, so Dad had talked to him while we were planning the move and made arrangements to buy a bike from him. We travelled through the night up the M1 motorway. It was a 440-kilometre trip from Worthing to Southport and we had made it about two-thirds of the way when we pulled in for a rest in a place called Nuneaton.

Our family had driven to race meetings all over Australia and it wasn't unusual for us to pull over in the middle of the night to sleep in the car. Dad had no idea that in England you can't just pull up at the side of the road like you can in Australia. You can't even stop overnight at the service stations; we tried but were kicked out by a parking attendant telling us we had to pay him to park there. We ended up driving around a village looking for somewhere to stop and this guy flagged us down, came over to the window and asked if we were travellers. We said we were, thinking, Well, we're travelling around in a van, of course we're travellers, not understanding that 'travellers' meant gypsies! He said to let him jump in and he'd show us how to get to his uncle's place, where we could camp. It sounded promising but when we got there the camp was like a scene straight from one of my favourite movies, *Snatch*, with Brad Pitt playing the gypsy fighter. This was the real thing: washing machines all over the place, dogs running around, clothes hanging up between trees and a few bonfires on the go. Dad wasn't bothered, saying, 'We'll just pull in and we'll be right!' I'm sure we would have been, but there was no way Mum and I wanted to stop there, so with a 'thanks, but no thanks' the guy hopped out and Dad kept driving. Eventually we came across a quiet industrial estate so we took our chances and found a hidden corner where we could sleep for a few hours, then we drove up to Ian Newton's the next day.

Ian, or Newt, as he was nicknamed, turned out to be a good bloke. He remembers us pulling up at his place: 'We'd spoken on the phone and Colin had sent a deposit over for the bike, but coming all the way from Australia, to be honest, I wasn't sure they were going to turn up. Next thing they pulled up at the workshop in this tatty yellow van with an old caravan hanging off the back and I thought, Wow, this is proper rough and ready. I showed them the bike and they were just really excited to get their hands on it. I asked Colin where they were going to be based and he said, "Well, I was hoping you might have a word with an Aprilia dealer somewhere in the Midlands so we can base ourselves there, maybe they'll give us a corner of the garage or something." I told him that might work in Australia but over here space is tight and nobody is going to just give you the corner of a workshop. But I had plenty of room so I told them they could set up at my place until they got sorted out. I told Colin they would need three things if they were going to succeed over here: talent, luck and money. He said, "The boy has the talent and hopefully we'll get some luck, but we don't have any money." Essentially they were prepared to put everything they had into Casey's racing and live on next to nothing.'

Newt not only gave us workshop space, he also found us a site on a farm not far from his place in Southport, where we could park the caravan. The weather wasn't any warmer than London. It was snowing and the heater in the caravan didn't work very well so we were freezing most of the time but we had somewhere to live, a bike and had made a friend so things were looking up – sort of! We'd arrived in England too early for the race season but that was part of the plan. I'd still not had any serious practice on a road bike to speak of, so we'd wanted to get to the UK as soon as possible and start testing. Now we knew where we were based the next step was for Mum and Dad to find themselves a job.

Because we had arrived in the UK earlier than we'd been planning, we had much less money than we'd have liked. Mum and Dad had intended to sell our house but after a lot

of thought they'd decided to keep it and rent it out to Kelly.
Then we had a disaster. Not long before we left, the house
burned down. Dad will tell you he'd been trying to save so
hard that he cut back on everything: 'I'd insured the house for
less than the insurance company reckoned it was worth, so we
had a big problem getting the money back. We got something,
but nowhere near its true value. Luckily, we still had the land
and another small place that we had rented out so we were at
least able to hang onto that and retain some capital, which we
knew we'd need at a later date.'

We'd left Australia with a fair amount of money but it didn't
go far. The exchange rate at the time wasn't good, about $3 to
£1. By the time we bought the van, the caravan and the bike,
there wasn't much left so we had to live as frugally as possible
to stretch the money out. We'd bought one-way tickets to get
to the UK and the plan was if things didn't work out we could
sell the bike to get back home.

I didn't even want to think about that possibility so it was
important to start testing as soon as we could. We took the
bike down to a local track in Wigan called Three Sisters,
where for a fee of around £5 you could pretty much ride all
day. Of course it was still the middle of winter in England so
I was riding around in the snow and sleet, trying to get used
to the bike as it slipped around underneath me on the frozen
bitumen, but I loved the track and would have ridden there
every day if I could. We had a few more runs at Three Sisters
before taking part in the official pre-season tests at Donington

Park and Mallory Park, where Newt introduced me to my first friend in the UK, Chaz Davies.

Chaz was the favourite for the Superteen championship. He says now: 'There was honestly just me and a couple of others I thought were going to be quick. I didn't know anything about Casey or even that he was going to be there, but I remember at the Donington test I found myself behind this guy in white leathers thinking I definitely wasn't catching him quickly enough. I wasn't happy because it was the start of the season and I realised there was an unexpected contender to deal with.'

I was pleased with how things went during testing and in the first race at Mallory I was fast. My riding style was pretty unorthodox for a road racer but it seemed to work well there and I was able to beat Chaz. I remember people being really shocked that I was backing it in at the hairpin because nobody had done that on a Superteen bike before. It was the only way I knew how to ride. I thought, That's what you do, isn't it? In the second round at Brands Hatch I qualified on pole by more than a second and lapped nineteen of thirty-two riders in the race, finishing 10 seconds clear of Chaz to take my second win from as many races.

By the time that first race came around Mum had managed to get a job in one of those roadside tea and coffee vans in a village near Southport called Scarisbrick, and Dad had found a part-time job at Blacks motorcycle shop in Southport. He was earning £40 a day but could only work three or four days a week because I had to go racing, so a lot of weeks he could earn £120 at the most. It cost us £150 in fuel just to drive down to Brands and back, so we were already dipping into what was left of our savings.

With baked beans at 9p a tin and bread for 15p a loaf we were eating enough beans on toast to last a lifetime. On very rare occasions we would treat ourselves to a full English breakfast with sausages, fried eggs and all the extras. A 'full English breakfast' still goes down as one of my all-time favourite meals.

In the Superteens there was £250 available for a win, twice what Dad could earn in a week, so there was a certain pressure for me to bring it home.

I know Mum and Dad didn't want me to take that worry on, but it was impossible not to because they'd put so much of their finances into moving overseas for me. Dad says: 'It didn't matter if it didn't work out, and we tried to make sure Casey knew that. If it happened it happened, if it didn't it didn't. My view was, What's the worst that can happen? I was still young enough to come home and buy another house if I wanted to, or get a caravan and travel around Australia, finding work along the way. That's the way we felt and that's what we told Casey but I know it was a big driving force for him, not to let us down. We all knew it but there was nothing we could do to change it. It was obvious.'

Having this responsibility to put food on the table is not a normal situation for a fourteen-year-old kid, but I tried not to think about it and to do my own thing. Once I was on the track it never even crossed my mind. I had a job to do, which was to win motorbike races, and that was the most normal thing in the world to me.

After the success at Mallory we were approached by a guy from a company called Lloyd Lifestyle, one of the UK's biggest importers of motorcycling equipment, saying they were interested in a sponsorship arrangement. When we asked Newt about them he said we should talk to them because they were a good family company. Lloyds wanted me to join their team and become a third rider alongside Craig Jones and John Lloyd, son of the company owner, George Lloyd. They offered us £5000 cash, a fortune to us at the time, but Dad told them he'd have to think about it. They couldn't believe it when we didn't jump at it. They then offered to pay our bills, entry fees and all sorts of stuff but again Dad said he wasn't sure and that he'd let them know.

Eventually, after the third round at Donington when I qualified second but crashed out of the lead after a couple of laps in half-wet-half-dry conditions, Lloyds came back with a fresh offer, whereby they would also employ Dad to run the team and do some delivery work for them. So in addition to the five grand cash Dad also had a job, a team to run and a van to drive, and I had a new set of leathers and a helmet from Lloyd's own brand, OGK. When we drove over to the company headquarters in Penrith to pick up the gear I was so excited about my new leathers that I wore them in the van all the way back to Southport and went straight round to Newt's house to show him.

Dad was proving to be a pretty hard negotiator and he didn't cut much slack when it came to dealing with me, either. Even though he said we could go back to Australia at any point I was never under the impression we were in England on holiday. Ever since I was little he'd told me that if we didn't go into a race to win then there was no point us even being there. Sometimes he'd mean that loosely because we might have a bike that was only capable of tenth place, in which case fourth can be better than a win. It's a weird thing, but in racing you can outperform the guy who gets to stand on top of the podium without actually beating him.

Going to the UK changed things for all of us. Dad could see I had the talent – we were up against some very good riders and I was beating them – so what had at times been just a dream was looking more and more like a real possibility to us. We both knew I had to take every opportunity and he encouraged me to do just that. At this point things were getting serious. Dad used to say, 'If you want to become World Champion you can't be *that* much better than local competition,' holding his finger and thumb an inch apart. 'You have to be *this* much better,' he'd say, holding his arms wide open.

Dad confirms this feeling still today: 'I know it's a harsh way to look at things but that's the difference between a champion and the rest. Just look at the careers of Dani Pedrosa and Jorge Lorenzo. Dani had Alberto Puig and Jorge had his old man, both of them hard as nails. If you want to make it to the top I think it takes somebody with an unforgiving view on life to help get you there. So I said those things to Casey, particularly when we went to the UK, because to keep moving up a level he couldn't just be happy with winning a race. If he wasn't winning by a margin that represented his maximum performance then he wasn't showing people how much better he was than the rest.'

There's no denying that Dani, Jorge and I became successful with that kind of upbringing and sometimes you probably do need it. As far as I'm concerned Alberto was nowhere near as tough on Dani as my dad was on me or Jorge's dad was on him. That kind of intensity and expectation puts a lot of extra pressure on a father–son relationship that isn't always healthy. We definitely had our moments and there were a few major blow-ups to come. But at the time, rightly or wrongly, it was proving to be a good system for us and I was eager to continue impressing my dad and others with my performances on the track.

M y first race as a Lloyds rider was in the fourth round at Thruxton, where I qualified second to my new teammate Jonesy and missed out on the win by 0.078 seconds

to a guy named Rob Butterworth. In the next round at
Snetterton I qualified on pole by more than a second clear
of Chaz and then beat him in a ten-lap race, which didn't go
down well with him or his parents, and some of that blew
back on Newt.

Newt says: 'To the other parents it was starting to look
dodgy. I was running the championship but I had this kid
racing out of my workshop and he was blowing the other kids
away. You can't imagine how much they bitched to me about
it, it was horrendous. They were convinced I was giving him
special parts that their kids weren't getting. They kept making
me pull the bike apart and everything. The Davies were a
lovely family but they were as bad as anybody. Chaz had been
"Rookie of the Year" in 1999 and in fairness he would probably
have won the series easily in 2000 but for this Aussie kid, who
had arrived out of nowhere. It was hard for them to take.'

I qualified a second clear of Chaz again for the next race
at Oulton Park, only to crash while chasing him for the lead,
but a first and a second in a double round at Cadwell Park in
August meant that despite not scoring in two of the rounds I
had closed the gap at the top of the championship to twenty-
four points with four races remaining. That gap shrank by
another ten points thanks to two more wins at Mallory and
Cadwell, where I won by 8 seconds in an eight-lap race.

Newt continues: 'Casey was beating them in the slow
corners; that's where he really excelled, which is why he loved
it so much at Three Sisters. Whereas other kids would just get

through them because they were no fun and you can't make up much time, Casey used to really focus on them. He'd slide in, get the bike turned and power out. At the bottom of the mountain at Cadwell he was unbelievable. He must have been three miles per hour quicker through there. But the most impressive thing was how fast he could be on the first lap. He wasn't doing lap records but he'd be close to them as soon as the flag dropped and that's where he'd win the race. He would just explode through the first few corners and you'd think, How is he doing that? I guess it came from his days in dirt-track, when the races only lasted three or four laps. Everybody knew that once he got away they weren't going to catch him. Casey was a laidback kid then but put a crash helmet on him and his eyes would glaze over. It sounds stupid but I'm serious, he was in a different world. His focus was amazing.'

The level of competition between Chaz and me, not to mention the increasing tension between our parents, finally began to affect our friendship. It was a real shame because we had become good friends and it was great to have someone my own age to hang out with. His family lived in a big old barn in the middle of the country on the English–Welsh border and they'd invited us down to visit not long after we met. They had a great track at the side of their house where we could race karts and minibikes and we could go off into the nearby forests to shoot air rifles. That was the closest I had been to everything I missed about Australia since we'd left.

Chaz knew how much I liked being at his place: 'I guess coming to our place was a bit of a holiday for Casey after living in a caravan with his mum and dad for months on end. He was such a country kid; there were some things I couldn't believe. I remember once we were hiking out in the forest and he took a cup, scooped some water out of an old tractor rut in the ground and knocked it back. I was like, "What the hell are you doing?" and he just said, "Well, it looks clean to me!" Stuff like that, you don't really see but it's quite natural to him. I'd never even met an Australian before so it was pretty cool to me. But his determination stood out straight away. It didn't matter if we were trying to throw a stone or playing PlayStation, everything was a competition. It sort of brought out more competition in me as well, because it was a case of surrendering or at least trying to challenge him! Unfortunately, when it came to racing, he was just too fast and it got too competitive between us. We ended up barely speaking to each other for the second half of that season.'

Once Chaz and I fell out, it turned into a bit of a lonely summer, but Kelly had given me a copy of Bryce Courtenay's *The Power of One* so I read a lot around this time. I'm not a huge reader but I love that book. 'First with your head, then with your heart' isn't a bad philosophy to live by. I also read all the Harry Potter books as they came out. But I still spent most of my time on a bike. We moved into a static caravan a couple of kilometres away from Newt's place and I used to ride my pushbike down the canal path to his and Myra's house for my breakfast, then spend the day at his workshop or fishing in the canal from the back of a narrow boat owned by one of his friends. The lady next door used to bake cakes and scones and I'd go round and pick up some fresh ones to take back home to the caravan.

Ian Newton remembers around that time we got a fax machine and I wanted to test it out: 'Casey sent a fax through to the office to see if it was working, something along the lines of, "I'm going to be Aprilia Superteen Champion 2000". I wrote back saying, "You can talk the talk but can you walk the walk?" He sent me a fax straight back that simply read, "I'm going to RUN the walk." We were only having a laugh but it's something that always stuck in my head because that's exactly what he did!'

Things were going really well in the Superteens and Lloyds agreed to help us buy a 125 so we could contest the final three rounds of the British Championship. We bought the bike from Mark Hodgson, father of Neil Hodgson, who was British Superbike Champion at the time and would go on to win the World Superbikes a couple of years later. Mark was actually running Leon Camier in the 125s but he also sold second-hand bikes and parts from his place in nearby Burnley, so we used to go over there and have a look through his bits and pieces, maybe buy a few things. He had the nickname 'Flask and Sandwiches' because he liked talking, so you knew that when you went over to his place you were going to be there for a while! Mind you, it's fair to say that my dad likes a chat too, so I'm sure they were as bad as each other.

Just like we had done back in Australia we rode pretty much any event we could get into: practice days, club days – you name it, we were there, either on the Superteen bike or the 125. On one occasion we went to Three Sisters and there was an inter-club 'Celtic Challenge' going on, England versus Ireland. After I'd been out on the track for a few laps one of the Irish guys came over to where we were working on the bike.

'Jaysus, kid, you came past me so fast I thought you were a feckin' rabbit!' he said. 'Are you Irish by any chance?'

'No, I'm Australian,' I replied.

'Hmm. But your grandmother was Irish, wasn't she?'

I suddenly realised what he was getting at. 'Oh yeah! Good old Grandma was Irish!' I said.

That was enough for him and we agreed I would ride for their team. On the Saturday we were doing pretty well, I won all my races and the Irish boys held up their end. On the Sunday morning we turned up, ready to race again, but it was pretty clear my new teammates had enjoyed a good night's 'craic', as they called it. One of them hadn't slept because they'd set his mattress on fire, another had blood pouring down his face because he'd fallen down a hill. Some of them tried to ride but most of them were in no fit state, so they had to send me out there to hold the whole thing together. I set the outright circuit record that day and won every race apart from the last one, when I crashed because I was so exhausted.

Somehow the scorers worked out that England won but given how many races we'd won, I wonder if they added it up right.

Not long after that we took the 125 over to Northern Ireland to a meeting at Kirkistown, organised by the father of a racer named Marty Nutt, who had a travel agency over there and was doing a lot of bike promotions. We told the organisers I was fifteen, even though I was only fourteen. We'd already learnt at Three Sisters the Irish are a pretty laidback bunch! I was riding against Ian Lougher, a famous Irish road racer, and other guys from the British Championship, and I was probably a bit out of my depth. We had a lot of trouble with the bike because it had a carbon-kevlar tank on it and the jets kept blocking up with bits of fibre. I had a couple of crashes, knocked myself out and busted my ankle up but got the chance to race with some fast guys and started to understand where we needed to improve.

My first 125cc British Championship race was at Mallory Park on 17 September 2000. We qualified eighth, just behind Leon Camier on the outside of the second row, but I got to the front on the first lap and ended up fighting all the way to the line with Christopher Martin and Stuart Easton, setting a new circuit record on the way to second place behind Martin.

The following weekend we went down to Brands Hatch where I qualified fourth in the dry, with Leon Haslam on pole. Leon was already racing in the World Championship by then so he was a good measuring stick for us. On the Sunday it poured with rain and I had a problem with my visor steaming up but I still managed to finish second to Leon, which was a big boost because I felt that without the visor issue, we could have fought for the win.

Two weeks later we headed back to Donington for the final round of the British Championship, which was also the final round of the Aprilia Superteens. Chaz was leading the Superteens by nine points, meaning that if I won he had to take second to make sure of the title. I qualified on pole on the Friday, with Chaz in third, and I made an early break on a damp track with a drying line. Chaz would normally have been comfortable in second place but unfortunately for him he got tangled up with a rider taking his chances in the mixed conditions and on the very last lap he was forced wide onto the wet part of the track. He crashed, handing me the championship by sixteen points.

Watching a competitor crash out wasn't how I liked to win but that is motor racing and winning the Aprilia Superteen Championship was a great day for me. I also qualified on pole position for the 125 race, which would take place the following day. On the Sunday morning the sun came out and I led for the opening few laps in the dry but just didn't have the pace to outrun Stuart Easton and he beat me by just over a second.

As the Aprilia Superteen Champion I was invited to the end-of-season awards dinner, which was formal dress. I didn't have a suit so Lloyds hired one for me. Newt helped us out too: 'I bought Casey a pair of dress shoes because he didn't own any. I remember that year I used to open the back door in the morning to let the dogs out and most days Casey would be standing there, waiting to come in for some breakfast. The first time I showed him where the cereal was he started examining the different boxes. It seemed a bit fussy to me so I asked him what he was doing – he was actually checking the dates, to make sure he was eating the oldest stuff first. Any other kid would have dived straight in without even thinking about such a thing. That's what he was like, though: polite, humble, just a great little kid.'

——— — — —

My performances in those last few British Championship rounds had caught the attention of a few people, including Mario Rubatto, who was actually working as a chassis engineer for one of the other riders, Jason DiSalvo, and Mario had previously run Grand Prix teams with a lot of success. The previous year, when we were in Australia, Ant West's dad, Tony, had kindly offered to hand my resumé out

Me and Dad on Kelly's 50cc in 1986. I was mighty happy on that bike! Grandpa is in the background and Mum is taking the photo.

When I wasn't on a bike I was playing with our cattle dog, Midge, hanging out with Kelly or spending time developing my other obsession – fishing. I started both young!

Dad and Midge tried to catch me – so I just had to go faster!

I like that! Checking out a 125 at Lakeside Park, Brisbane, in June 1990.

Here I am at Hatcher's on my first race day in June 1990. I'm wearing an old leather jacket of Kelly's that Mum added my name to.

Lining up for my first race at Mike Hatcher's. Dad and Kelly are giving me a pep talk because I was nervous at all the attention. Once I was racing I was fine.

I took my racing very seriously from the beginning. This one time, I was more than happy to copy my heroes and celebrate with a bottle of bubbly when I won. I didn't drink any, just showered the bike and myself.

At Mike Hatcher's in October 1991, just before my sixth birthday.
Here I am following Australian Superbike Champion Aaron Slight.
I was determined to keep up.

Me and Kelly selling guava jam at our roadside stall outside our place on the Tamborine Mountain road.

These were the bikes I competed on, and the trophies I won, at the national dirt and long track championships in 1997.

Not that I was counting, but by the time I was nine the pool room was getting crowded!

One of my first track-side interviews.

The transition from dirt to road racing took none of my enthusiasm away; I aimed to get better and better. I was fourteen years old and just wanted to ride bikes. I didn't know what was about to happen to stop me in my tracks!

Me and Mum enjoying our first white Christmas in the UK. Dad was behind the camera this time.

When we first arrived in the UK we lived in a small caravan with an annex. We moved from there to a static caravan (more like a mobile home) for five months, then, when we got the deal with Lloyds, we moved into a small granny flat. We had the part of the building with the chimney. It was tiny!

to a few key people in Europe and by coincidence Mario was one of the guys who'd taken a look at it.

Mario Rubatto: 'I saw Casey ride the 125 for the first time in the wet at Brands and I was blown away. He was unbelievable, the most talented rider I had ever seen. You didn't need to be an expert to know that you were looking at something very special. I immediately rang my wife and said, "Find the resumé of that Australian boy, see if it is the same one!" Of course it was, so I went to his father and told him that Casey stood no chance of progressing if he stayed in Britain because they were only interested in promoting their own riders, but that I had a bike and a race truck back in Germany that we could take to the final couple of rounds of the Spanish Championship if they wanted. All he had to do was provide the tyres and £5000 to cover the costs and I would supply the rest. We made a deal right there and then.'

Dad and I liked Mario's style and knew this was a big opportunity for us, even if it had come a bit sooner than we expected. Dad says, 'Mario and I didn't always see eye to eye on everything, but he was a great help to us and is still a good friend.'

The British Championship was pretty competitive, but the Spanish series was the next level up and had already proven to be a stepping stone to world level for a lot of riders. Most people we spoke to thought it was too soon for me, but we decided to trust we were making the right decision and try our luck on the European mainland.

Lloyds agreed to pay the travel costs, Dad scraped some money together and the three of us headed over to Germany to meet up with Mario, jumping into the back of his race truck to drive 1800 kilometres all the way down to Albacete in the south of Spain. The bike was a standard Honda RS125, like the one I'd been riding in the UK, with a couple of bits and pieces bolted on it. The truck had a living area in the front and some bunks in the back. Mario also brought along a mechanic called Hans.

Things went well in practice at Albacete and I quickly got used to the track, which had some of the tight and slow corners I liked. The biggest problem was choosing the tyres. Dunlop did three kinds of rubber for the 125: 'B', 'C' and 'D'. 'B' was the softest compound, which we ran in the British Championship; 'C' was a medium compound; and obviously 'D' was the hardest. We were running the 'C's in practice at Albacete but Mario reckoned we'd have to use the 'D's over race distance so he made me go out and test them. I was losing the front all over the place, I just couldn't keep the bike upright and I thought, There's no way I can use these things in the race. So we went with the 'C's and even though they went off pretty quickly I was going well, running in the top five when the organisers stopped the race for a crash.

Pretty much everybody else went in and put new tyres on, but of course we didn't have any spares because we couldn't afford them. So I had to go back out on the same rubber, or what was left of it. The white of the cord was actually showing through and I ended up dropping a couple of places and finishing fifth in a race won by Toni Elías. Afterwards one of the other riders must have been complaining about his tyres because his team manager dragged him into our pit box to show him what I was riding on. He shouted at the rider in Spanish, something like, 'Now don't bust my balls!'

In the next round at Jerez we decided to test out the 'D' compound again since we knew the 'C's had no chance of lasting a race distance. It wasn't until we checked the pressure that we realised they had about 70 pounds in them, which meant that at Albacete they'd basically been pumped up enough to pop them on the rim of the wheel but hadn't been let down again. We had major engine problems in the race and only finished sixteenth. Afterwards I pushed the bike back to the pits. It had so little compression that I didn't even notice it was in gear.

Thankfully I'd done enough in that first race at Albacete to catch the attention of Alberto Puig, a tough and uncompromising 500cc Grand Prix winner from Spain whom I'd watched race against Mick Doohan a couple of times on television back in Australia. Alberto's competitive career had effectively come to a premature end when he slid under the air fence and hit the barriers after a high-speed crash in turn one at Le Mans, badly breaking his leg.

He was now dedicating his time to finding fresh Spanish talent on behalf of the national telecommunications company Telefónica Movistar and MotoGP's television and commercial rights holders, Dorna. After bringing some pretty special kids through the Spanish Championship that season (including a previously unknown young rider called Daniel Pedrosa) they had decided to open the project up to riders from other countries for the next campaign.

In the stern and abrupt style we would soon become very familiar with, Alberto limped over to my dad in the pit lane at Albacete and simply said, 'Who is this boy?'

'This is my son, Casey Stoner,' Dad replied.

'Well, I want him to race for me next year in the Spanish Championship,' said Alberto.

It's fair to say we didn't know much about Grand Prix racing at this point but one thing we did know was that you don't say no to Alberto Puig.

CHAPTER 5

VIVA ESPAÑA

After just a year in the UK the idea of relocating to Spain was daunting, but in a way it was similar to the decision we'd made during my dirt-track days, moving down from the Gold Coast to the Hunter Valley area where the competition was stronger. We already had an agreement in place with Lloyds to contest the British Championship but we knew the real competition was at the Spanish Championship in terms of riders, bikes and teams, plus the majority of the Spanish circuits were on the Grand Prix calendar, so it became our number-one priority.

With the way the calendar worked out we figured I could ride in both championships but we'd have to miss three rounds of the British Championship. We were concerned this would be an issue for Lloyds, but luckily they were very understanding and supportive sponsors. In fact, they backed our decision, helping us financially so we could buy an old motorhome from Mario and keep it on the road for thousands of kilometres as we travelled backwards and forwards from the UK to mainland Europe. They also helped pay for living expenses.

It would have been almost impossible for Mum, Dad and me to achieve what we did without George and Cath Lloyd helping us and we developed a great personal relationship with the Lloyd family. I really enjoyed spending time with George, he had a great sense of humour, and John became a friend and a teammate. George passed away in September 2012 and I was very sad to hear of his death. I will always be grateful for the support he and Cath gave us in those early days of my career.

Relationships like this are pretty rare in the world of racing and for a kid like me, spending all my time moving from one racetrack to another in a motorhome with my parents, it wasn't easy to make friends, especially with people my own age. Even back in Australia I never really hung around in big groups and I hadn't been to school for a couple of years because we kept up the home-schooling so when I did interact with people it was usually one on one. It was the same in the UK and to be honest, sometimes I struggled to fit in because I found the English sense of humour a lot different from what I was used to. Everyone else seemed to be a bit more quick-witted than

I was and if the joke was on me often I wasn't too sure how to take it. It definitely took me some time to get used to certain things.

Luckily, as well as inviting me over to Spain, Alberto had also approached Chaz Davies and Leon Camier to form part of an eight-man line-up supported by Telefónica Movistar and Dorna that also included a kid called Jascha Büsch from Germany, and Spanish riders Julian Simon, Joan Lascorz, Jordi Torres and David Salom. Chaz and I still weren't really back on the best of terms but being thrown together in difficult circumstances helped us quickly patch up our differences.

In the end Chaz and I felt the same way. Chaz says: 'When we went to Spain we didn't speak Spanish, we didn't know anyone and there was me, Leon and Casey. We all depended on each other a little bit. We travelled together and our parents shared rental cars, because obviously we had to pay for that sort of stuff ourselves, and we had to make the best of it. We all had different experiences of it. Casey and Julian Simon were automatically selected to be the guys to compete for the championship, because they showed they were fast straight away. But I think it was a good opportunity for all of us.'

At the start we were all given identical bikes but I was 1.5 seconds quicker than the other guys in the first test so they gave me an updated air box and exhaust. Basically, if you showed the potential they gave you support to see what else you could do and whether you were capable of running at the front. Simon was even smaller than Dani Pedrosa at the time so he could also make the bike look better than it was, especially in terms of power, so he got a few extra bits and pieces too. I think I ended up with a 1998 kit on my bike, although this was in 2001 so they were still a long way off Grand Prix specs. Given my history of makeshift bikes I wasn't complaining!

Our first race that year was in the British Championship at Donington, where I managed to qualify on pole by 1.3 seconds from Leon and win the race by 5.8 seconds in front of a guy named Paul Robinson with Leon in third. As well as the win, I got to meet former Grand Prix World Championship rider Barry Sheene that weekend. Barry was working as a racing commentator and he interviewed me for Australian television. Barry Sheene was a rider I looked up to, for his talent and his honesty. When he was riding, he was known to speak out if he thought safety was being compromised. I respected that. And he was fast, something I was determined to be.

Two weeks later we were at Silverstone, where I set a new pole record by a second in qualifying and then won a close race with Leon by half a second. I only managed to qualify third in the third round at Snetterton but we got ourselves sorted out for the race. I took the lead on the second lap and went on to break the circuit record, winning by more than 20 seconds. After three races I had three wins and a twenty-eight-point championship lead over Robinson, with Leon another point behind.

I'd wanted to use the number 66 when I raced, but another rider had taken it. Number 66, or 166 if there had to be three digits, had always been my number in dirt-track because Dad had used number 6. I had run 66 in the Aprilia Superteens but it had been taken in the British Championship so I'd used 48, which is what I was given. For the Spanish series Alberto had block-booked all the twenties for his riders and I was given the number 27. It was the number I would keep from then on.

The fourth round clashed with the opening round of the Spanish Championship, so instead of heading to Oulton Park in Cheshire, Leon, Chaz and I left for Jarama, Madrid.

The eight of us were all in awe of Alberto Puig. Chaz remembers how tough Alberto was: 'Not tough to deal with or to talk to, but the conversation began and ended with what was going on at the track and he runs a strict program there. In the second round at Albacete, Camier got a bad start. "What happened?" Alberto asked him, so Leon said, "Somebody in front of me bogged it off the line and I had to back off and I lost loads of ground ..." Alberto looked at him and said "You must hit him!" So it was like, okay, we're here for racing, whatever it takes.'

I was definitely only there for the racing and I think Alberto liked that. I started the season with the standard bike from testing, with a few small upgrades, but managed to finish third behind two Spanish kids – Ángel Rodríguez, who was already scoring points in the World Championship by then, and Héctor Faubel. After that we stayed on in Spain for the next round back down at Albacete, where I managed to beat

Rodríguez for the win, and then we headed back to the UK for the British Championship. I went on to win the fifth round at Brands Hatch by almost 16 seconds after setting a new pole record in qualifying.

Beating a current Grand Prix rider like Rodríguez might have attracted the attention of a few people but we honestly never looked at it like that or started thinking about what a result like that meant. I know it sounds strange, but for me it was all about doing my best on the day with the bike that was underneath me, nothing more than that. I never try to look too far ahead or too much into the past. There is no point and it doesn't interest me, probably another reason why I resisted writing a book for so long!

I managed to set another pole record in the next round at Thruxton but we were having a problem with the bike and the air box kept filling up with fuel. After two laps of warm-up on the morning of the race it spilled fuel all over the rear tyre and I had a huge high-side crash, literally snapping my bike into two pieces. There was no way we could fix it in time for the race and Paul Robinson, who had finished third in the race we missed at Oulton, took third again to cut my lead to eleven points.

We went back to Spain in mid-July for the Valencia race but things didn't go so well. It rained in practice and unfortunately the team didn't have proper wet-track tyres. I crashed and hurt my hip. The rain stopped and the track dried out for the race, but the painkilling injections I'd been given to get me on the bike started to wear off and I went from first backwards through the field.

Along with Rodríguez, Faubel and my teammate Julian Simon there was another rider at the front in the Spanish Championship by the name of Jorge Lorenzo. I didn't know much about him at the time, but he'd just turned fourteen so he was eighteen months younger than me and clearly very fast. He finished third in that race at Valencia and then second in the next round at Albacete, where I struggled to place sixth because of a chatter problem that was so bad it left me with blisters on my hand like you wouldn't believe.

In between those two races we also took part in three more rounds of the British Championship and won all three quite comfortably: at Oulton Park by more than 6 seconds; at Knockhill by 11 seconds; and at Cadwell by 9 seconds. Cadwell was a particularly good weekend because we set a new lap record in qualifying and in the race I was 2.4 seconds clear after the first lap. After four laps the gap was 6 seconds and I stretched it to 9 in front of Chaz (who took second place) by the finish.

Dad has a pretty good story from that weekend at Oulton. 'It was wet and Casey completely lost confidence. I don't know why and neither does he, still to this day. When it came to qualifying he said to me, "Put the old fairings on, Dad, I'm either going to fix this or I'm going to crash." He went out and on his second lap he was 5 seconds clear of everybody else. He came straight back in and sat the rest of the session out.

By the end he was still on pole by 2.5 seconds. We put the new fairings back on for the race.'

Having achieved some stronger results, Leon had left the Spanish Championship to concentrate on the British. He was now placing second in the championship but still sixty points behind me with four races to go. The next two rounds coincided with the Spanish Championship but I didn't really care about missing those races. My goal was never to be British Champion, or Spanish Champion, or even 125cc or 250cc World Champion for that matter. My dream was always to be 500cc World Champion because for me it was the only title that mattered. Whatever we felt was the next step towards achieving that was the step we took. Even though it was still a distant dream at this point, at least in my head, Dad would again say, 'Aim for the stars and if you hit the moon you're doing pretty well.'

It was important to keep testing ourselves against the best possible competition and we got the opportunity to step up another level that July with a wildcard entry for the British Grand Prix. Unfortunately, as they were still only fourteen, Chaz and Leon were too young to enter but I was fifteen so I could. Alberto invited me to ride for the Telefónica Movistar team as a fourth rider with Dani Pedrosa, Joan Olivé and Toni Elías, although I would have my standard bike and mechanics from the Spanish Championship as opposed to the factory Honda Grand Prix kit they were on. We had massive chatter problems we couldn't get rid of but in a wet session I finished

second, which felt really good. Another problem I had that
weekend was Alex De Angelis coming past me on the straight
and hitting my front brake lever, trying to give me a scare.
Alberto was furious and I can't say I was happy about it, either.
I finally struggled to seventeenth, which wasn't what I'd hoped
for. However, I wasn't really interested in the occasion itself or
the significance of riding in the World Championship for the
first time; for me it was always a stepping stone.

I made up for that poor result back in the Spanish
Championship. After the sixth placing at Albacete we went
back to Jarama in September for the fifth round of seven,
where I managed to take my second win. My bike had been
upgraded during the summer break and I won the race, beating
Faubel and Rodríguez by about 15 seconds and breaking the
lap record by 1.8 seconds. The previous record had been set
by Emilio Alzamora in 1999, the year he was 125cc World
Champion, and to break it was something special for two
reasons. First, Alzamora had become one of my favourite
riders; even though he didn't always have the best machinery,
he was always there at the front, always fighting in every race,
which was something I really looked up to. Secondly, the kit
I was riding on was actually older than the bike he'd been on
when he set the record two years before.

There wasn't another race in Spain until late November
so we went back to the UK with a chance to wrap up the
British Championship at Rockingham. Even though Leon had
reduced my lead to ten points after winning the two races I'd

missed I was still pleased to see him again. By this time Leon, Chaz and I had also become good friends with another racer in the British paddock, Andy 'Storka' Walker. Our parents used to call the four of us the 'Brat Pack' and the nickname has stuck to this day. Andy now works as Leon's manager and we try to get together pretty much every year either in Europe or Australia with our wives and partners. It doesn't matter where we are, we always have a good time together.

We'd been racking up a lot of kilometres driving back and forth from the UK and around Europe so we couldn't believe it when, after a ten-hour drive, we discovered a tiny kitten hiding out on top of the suspension unit of the motorhome. I'm not sure how he'd survived the journey and instead of naming him Lucky we decided on Flucky. I'll let you work that one out! It was nice having a pet again. Fez and Zef were long gone and it made it a bit more homely having Flucky around.

The focus, though, was always on the next race. I qualified fastest in mixed conditions on the Saturday at Rockingham and it rained heavily on the Sunday morning but by the time we lined up on the grid – me on pole, Leon second and Chaz on the outside of the front row in fourth – the track had started to dry. I doubt any of us were thinking about the championship at the time, we just wanted to beat each other. The three of us took off at the front and after the first lap we were almost 2 seconds clear of the rest of the pack. On the second lap Leon crashed, meaning that all I had to do to win the championship was finish second. Of course, second place didn't interest me so I battled with Chaz, swapping places on every lap.

With four laps to go Chaz lost control and went down right in front of me. I had nowhere to go but straight over the top of his bike. The race was over for both of us and realistically my championship chances also, as Leon was planning to race in the final round at Donington while I was flying back to Australia for my second wildcard ride with Alberto, this time at Phillip Island. While we were away Leon won the title by just three points after a fourth-place finish in that last race and I was really happy for him as he was my mate.

Almost two years after leaving Australia following the stonewalling by the AJRRA I was back in October 2001 to race a road bike for the first time in my home country, all thanks to the goodwill of a Spanish team. I know I said I don't really look forward or back but this was a big moment for Mum, Dad and me because despite the best efforts of some to hinder my progression in racing, we didn't back down and they hadn't stopped us.

One of the most memorable moments of this trip back to Australia was the chance to meet one of my all-time heroes, Peter Brock. Peter was a motor-racing legend, one of Australia's best-known and most-loved V8 drivers. His achievements are too many to list here but he has to be considered the most successful driver in Australia's motor-racing history. Peter came up to me in the pits to introduce himself and say hello and ended up spending heaps of time chatting to me and Dad. It gave me a real boost to have someone like him take an interest in me and give encouragement to a young bloke just starting out.

Another man who I didn't know until this trip, and who would go on to become a major force in our lives, was James Strong. At the time he was Chief Executive of Qantas. James had started out as a lawyer and had risen to the top of the Australian business world. He made his mark in many successful businesses but as successful and connected as he was he never judged anyone on their job or appearance. He was the most unpretentious, kind man and he would become a mentor and adviser to both me and Dad. He guided Dad on many business decisions and helped us both deal with the complexities and stresses that come with professional motor racing and sponsorship deals. That race at Phillip Island gave me much more than just a competitive event, it helped introduce me to a lifelong friend.

The Phillip Island track is in a beautiful spot but on the 125 the layout wasn't much fun because you were flat out everywhere. The key was to have trust in the middle of the corner, open the throttle and hope you were in the right spot. Actually finding the right spot takes a bit of experience and of course I had never been there before, unlike most of the guys I would be racing.

We were on the back foot from the start of the weekend. The chatter problems we'd suffered at Donington were particularly bad in the long corners. Dad worked out that the wheels were the source of the problem and once we changed them we dropped our lap times by almost 2 seconds. Unfortunately, we only had one set so I had to qualify on whatever was on the wheels at the time, finishing up nineteenth on the grid.

My start wasn't bad but I made a few mistakes in the early laps, trying to rush things too much, and even though I felt like I could have stayed with the front group of nine or ten riders a gap appeared and once it was there I couldn't close it down. They never got too far ahead but it was too late and my opportunity was gone. I still ended up battling in the second group with some experienced guys I'd only seen on TV, such as Gino Borsoi and Nobby Ueda.

They were passing each other in every corner and it was something I wasn't used to because in the Spanish and British championships I would be fighting one or two guys maximum, but now there was a whole bunch of competitive guys on good machinery ready to put up a fight. Nobby's and Gino's experience showed in the end and they positioned themselves well for the last lap, keeping me behind them in twelfth place, 17 seconds behind the winner, Youichi Ui.

I know most people would think racing in my home Grand Prix at fifteen years of age must have been a hugely exciting experience for me but that wasn't the case. I had a job to do and there was a lot of pressure to get a result if I wanted to secure a ride for 2002. There wasn't really any time for me to enjoy myself because there was so much at stake and the sacrifices we had already made had become my biggest source of motivation. Living in a caravan on the north-west coast of England in the middle of winter, 20,000 kilometres from home was hard enough, but even harder was the prospect that it could all be for nothing. I was never there to be a part of the process or to enjoy the experience. I was there to make something out of every opportunity because I was never sure if it would be my last one. That fear of not being offered a ride for the following season was a constant driving force in those early days.

Nowadays I see too many kids coming through behaving too relaxed, and too happy with what they have achieved already. I don't want them to be miserable but they have to understand what's at stake. Like anybody else in any other job you've got to be serious about it; you can't go out and party every night and turn up for work and expect to do your job right. It just doesn't happen. Racing is the same but unfortunately a lot of kids turn up, think they can ride on talent alone and if it happens it happens. If it doesn't they go home with their tail between their legs and they think nothing more of it. It doesn't seem to matter to them. It mattered to me!

From a technical point of view one of the main areas in which I felt I was lacking compared with the European kids was trailing the front brakes into the corners, which loads the front tyre and gives better grip and stability. It's a technique they were able to master from a much earlier stage than me because I came from dirt-track where you mainly use the rear brake, while they came through minibikes, where you use a lot of front. I had experimented with this as a kid but I just wasn't used to pushing the front tyre hard or at an angle and it took me a long time to get good at it – well into my MotoGP career.

My strength was in the way I could adapt to different circumstances: different bikes, tracks, tyres and weather conditions, which was all thanks to my background in dirt-track. I had spent hundreds of hours riding every different kind of surface imaginable – dirt tracks, oil tracks, speedway and bitumen – feet up, feet down, knee down and sideways. Almost every single minute of that time had been spent practising 'the right way', as Mum always insisted. In comparison with the guys I was now racing against I found myself equipped to ride around problems in a way that they couldn't. I could take a bike another kid couldn't ride and make it work.

The final round of the Spanish Championship was held at Jerez at the end of November. I was sixteen. The World Championship had finished by then so a bunch of the Grand

Prix boys came down and entered, as well as Andrea Dovizioso, who was European Champion, but I bolted and won by about 15 seconds. Rodríguez had already secured the title in the previous round at Valencia but my win gave me second in the championship.

It was good to prove to people like Alberto Puig that their faith in me had been worth it. Alberto recalls: 'He came to Spain and he was super fast initially, he was just lacking experience. We gave him a good bike and put him on a good package there. In the end we could not win the title because we had some problems in some races but he was the fastest rider out there, for sure. I remember after that year I went one day to Carmelo [Ezpeleta, CEO of Dorna] and said, "Listen, this guy is super good in my opinion and after this year racing in Spain with a 125cc Honda you must, you must, help him to go to MotoGP."'

Friends like Alberto were gold. It all comes back to the 'we' I refer to. If I was going to have any chance of becoming 500cc MotoGP Champion I needed help to get there.

CHAPTER 6

THE HARD ROAD

The next step in chasing the dream of racing in the 500cc World Championship was a big jump. With Alberto's help I was offered a place in Lucio Cecchinello's newly formed 250cc team, riding a semi-factory Aprilia, alongside David Checa, younger brother of the more well known Carlos.

It was a good ride but a big ask for a sixteen-year-old rookie to race a 250cc two-stroke Grand Prix prototype only two years after first road racing laps on an 80cc Moriwaki around a go-kart track. It was definitely pushing my limits but I was just one step away from the 500cc World Championship (by now rebranded as MotoGP and opened up to 900cc four-strokes) so I sure wasn't complaining. Most rookies make their entrance to world competition on a 125cc, but we didn't have that opportunity available so of course we were going to accept the offer that meant I was able to race.

Unfortunately my favourite number, 66, was again already taken, this time by the German rider Alex Hofmann, so we decided to stick with my number from the Spanish Championship, 27. That same year in the 125cc class Joan Olivé would be running number 25 and Dani Pedrosa number 26, so having the number 27 on the front of my bike was a subtle but nice way to maintain my association with Alberto and his team of riders and show my respect for him.

Alberto's involvement didn't stop at helping us find a team and it was through him that we also received an offer of sponsorship from Nolan helmets. Of course we already had a relationship with Lloyds that was very important to us and they had wanted to make the step up to GPs together to promote the OGK brand that we'd been supporting in the British and Spanish Championships. We really didn't want to leave Lloyds behind but the amount of travel we had in front of us meant that Dad couldn't really do other work anymore. We needed every penny we could get and Lloyds couldn't match the offer from Nolan and Nolan were prepared to take a big risk on a rider they knew little about. It was a hard decision but one we had to make.

Lucio agreed to cover costs for our flights to the races outside Europe and some other expenses, but we still had fuel, tolls and day-to-day living to pay for so the deal with Nolan was very important. It worked out at about €35,000 for the season and with a little extra cash from gear-maker Spidi for my leathers, which was paid to Lucio first, it meant we could just about cover our expenses for the year. Our existing motorhome didn't have the legs to cover the distances needed for another year but thankfully Spidi offered to lend us one of theirs, which had also seen plenty of miles but at least it had a bit of life left in the engine (we hoped).

We'd spent the European winter back in Australia. Mum and Dad had bought a mobile home that was based in a caravan park near Anna Bay, on the mid-north coast of New South Wales, so we had somewhere to stay when we came home. It is a beautiful area that has some really good fishing so was a great place to unwind but getting organised for the next season was always a challenge in a different time zone. It meant many early-morning phone calls. In early 2002 Dad and I flew back to Europe to finalise our arrangements and complete some pre-season testing on the 250cc before we jumped on a flight to Japan for the first race of the season at Suzuka. We met up with Chaz Davies and his dad, Pete, at a connecting airport. Chaz was also making his Grand Prix debut that season with one of the smaller Italian teams in the 125cc class and I remember boarding the plane together and comparing our new helmet designs. We were both looking forward to the weekend ahead.

Arriving in Japan was definitely a strange experience for a country kid like me. It was very different from the beaches around Anna Bay and the casual Australian lifestyle we were used to. The challenge of riding the 250 at a completely new circuit didn't scare me but it was definitely a huge learning curve. I qualified fifteenth, one place ahead of my new teammate David Checa, which I wasn't pleased with. I expected better of myself. Up until this point I'd been more often at the front of whatever category I had raced in and so I found it hard to accept I wasn't doing the same in the 250cc.

Things got worse on race day when it absolutely poured down with rain. As we sat on the start line, the standing water on the track continued to increase, which created an instant wall of spray that I was right in the middle of as we headed towards the tight right-hander at turn one. I could barely make out where I was going, let alone how the bike was feeling, but after surviving the chaos of the first corner I tried to find some space for myself on the run down to turn two, a tricky left-hander that tightens into a chicane. As I lifted my head up from behind the fairing and grabbed the brakes, someone moved across in front of me and I clipped their back wheel and went down. It's a harsh reality that in Grand Prix you can fly halfway around the world for a race and it can be all over within two corners.

My second 250cc race was on the other side of the world in South Africa and it didn't last much longer. This time I qualified much better, lining up on the outside of the second row in eighth place, only half a second off a front row start. Just like when I'd made my wildcard appearance at Phillip

Island, I knew I had the chance to run with the front guys and I was determined not to let them get away at the start and then spend all race struggling to catch up.

This time I was aggressive as soon as the lights went out. The entire front row ahead of me moved to the right to take a position on the outside of the track for the left-hand sweep into turn one and the way was cleared for me to hold my position on the inside, pass six guys and hit the apex in second place, right on the rear wheel of the championship favourite, Marco Melandri.

I knew that Marco was on a hard tyre but as he pushed his factory machine in the early stages I was able to hang on, matching him corner for corner until we crossed the line at the end of the first lap with just over a tenth of a second between us. Chasing hard behind us were a trio of experienced Italians – former 125cc World Champion Roberto Locatelli, Roberto Rolfo and Franco Battaini. The harder I chased Marco the more I ran wide and the more he edged ahead. By the end of the second lap he had increased his advantage to half a second.

I decided to stop focusing on Marco and concentrate on using my own braking markers, which had worked well for me in qualifying. What I didn't allow for was that with a full tank of fuel the bike weighed around ten kilos more than it had done in qualifying, so all my reference points were effectively no good. It was only a matter of time before things went wrong. As I went through the fast left over a slight crest at turn three the bike became unsettled by a bump and as I braked hard for the tight right-hander at turn four the extra load on the front made the suspension bottom out, the jolting impact causing the rear wheel to lift slightly off the ground.

With the bike already at an angle the rear moved to one side, the rubber bit hard on the tarmac as it came back down and drove even more force through the flexing chassis and suspension. When I grabbed the brakes again, trying not to plough straight into Melandri as he tipped into the corner ahead of me, the rear tyre flicked from one edge to the other and the bike loaded up and bucked before launching me into the air. It was a big crash but I think it looked more spectacular than what it was and at least I knew why it had happened. Despite how dramatic it looked, I only ended up with a scratch on my chin.

Crashes only ever scare me when I don't understand what happened. If I made a mistake and I knew what it was then I just made sure I didn't do it again. I might have been a bit more hesitant but I never let fear get the better of me. I guess that's why I continued to take risks because even if something wasn't right with the bike I would still push it. To become a champion you have to. Over the years this approach meant that I picked up a few bruises but I also learnt a lot about riding a bike when it wasn't perfect. The biggest lesson I learnt was not to be proud and blame the machine. You have to look at yourself and if you make a mistake hold your hands up and admit it, especially to yourself. You will never improve as a racer if you are constantly blaming the bike.

After the race, we flew back to Barcelona to meet Mum,
who'd arrived from Australia, and picked up the new (old)
motorhome, ready for the start of the European season. I was
feeling a little frustrated about the previous couple of races
but happy that I had learnt some valuable lessons already.
Since we didn't have a permanent home in between races
Alberto generously organised with his father for us to park
the motorhome at the Puig family home. This was a beautiful
property with a lot of land on the outskirts of a town called
Cardedeu, north-east of Barcelona. After so much travelling
it is always nice to have somewhere to go with some room to
relax. The Puigs had a motocross bike that I could use and I
quickly set up my own little track on their land.

Alberto Puig's father is a very kind man. Not only did he
allow us to camp at his place, he also found us an old car to buy
so that we could drive to the supermarket or take a day trip to
the beach. The small things like that really helped us through
and we'll always be extremely grateful to the Puig family, not
just for the belief Alberto showed in me as a young rider but
for the whole family's generosity away from the races.

Our 'new' home was a big American motorhome that Spidi
had previously used as a service vehicle. With Mum, Dad and
me in there along with everything we owned it felt pretty snug,
let me tell you. It can be a real challenge both travelling and
living in the confines of a motorhome. It is a small space with
kitchen, dining, seating and sleeping all almost on top of each
other. During the European summer it would get incredibly

hot inside and the air-conditioning didn't always work. One night at Mugello in Italy it was at least 35 degrees and it was like an oven. When we were travelling we had to sleep with all the windows closed and the home locked up tight so we didn't get robbed.

One night we were stopped at a service station in a big area used as an overnight stop by caravans and motorhomes. Thieves target places like this and use gas to make sure everyone inside is unconscious before they break in. The one time it happened to us they couldn't get inside because we were locked up like Fort Knox. The owners of three other vans parked near us weren't so lucky. While they lost money and passports all we had to deal with was a bit of a headache (though Mum thought it was the best sleep she'd had in ages!) and a stolen battery-powered scooter from the enclosed trailer.

The motorhome did the job, most of the time, but not without a few dramas along the way. The first was on the trip driving from Spain to Italy for the third round of the championship after a race at Jerez.

Dad remembers it well: 'It's a bloody long way from Jerez to Mugello, over 2000 kilometres, with some pretty hairy roads along the way. I was coming down the side of this mountain pass when the electrics went. Suddenly I had no lights or brakes. I didn't even have gears because it was automatic. In Australia it wouldn't have been a problem because all the big vehicles like that have air tanks and if the air supply stops the

brakes lock up. The American system is power assisted, like
a car; if you try to roll downhill without the engine running
and put the brakes on you get something but it's not much. So
there I was, standing on the brakes, arms wrapped around the
steering wheel and shouting out to poor Bronwyn and Casey,
who were fast asleep. They got the fright of their lives when
they woke up. Thankfully we got the thing stopped but it was
scary as hell.'

We got it going again but it stopped again on the motorway.
We had to call the police to help us tow it out of the way.

Dad stayed up late fixing it and finally we set off again.
He drove all night and he had a lot of cans of Red Bull to
keep him going. We got to Mugello in time for the Tuesday
morning test but it rained and so it was cancelled. That was
typical of Grand Prix, it was a hard slog just to give yourself a
chance of racing.

Our dramas on the road were nothing compared to the
trouble I was about to have on the track with the Aprilia. After
a fairly good weekend at Jerez, where I finished sixth after
qualifying seventh, I had back-to-back crashes at Le Mans and
Mugello and for the first time in my life doubt crept into my
mind. I had a really experienced crew chief, Massimo Biagini,
who'd worked with many top riders in the past and so when he
told me what he thought I was doing wrong I listened.

I'd already worked out that I wasn't like any rider Biagini
had worked with before. Perhaps because of my dirt-track
days, my skill set was different to European riders and I was

very sensitive to what was going on with the bike beneath me. For an engineer, like Massimo, whose relationship with a motorcycle is through a laptop computer, this can be a difficult concept to accept. Often the data would tell him one thing but I was telling him something else and sometimes people with a mind for science tend to rely on the numbers rather than a rider's instinct.

Being in a team means trusting each other and listening but that is a two-way street as far as I am concerned and I became frustrated that Massimo didn't seem to listen to what I had to say. The worst thing was that often the numbers weren't right and we'd go from one race to the next with a completely different setting. I would come in saying the bike felt completely unlike the previous week and Massimo would be insisting it was the same.

No matter how strong my self-belief was, as a rookie I couldn't help but question myself because someone with more experience was telling me I was wrong. Throughout my whole career I had been able to adapt to pretty much anything but I couldn't get the hang of this bike. It put me in a bad frame of mind, thinking I was never going to make it so there was no point in continuing. Coming into Grand Prix I guess I had this idea that everybody knew what they were doing. I had an experienced chief mechanic so I assumed things were going to move forward quickly for me. For a lot of that season I blamed myself that things weren't turning out. I couldn't understand why I didn't have speed, why I wasn't comfortable on the bike.

The team were supportive but having my instincts disregarded caused me to question my abilities and could very nearly have ruined my career.

Dad could see I was struggling: 'The last round of the year was at Valencia and Casey had another terrible result, finishing thirteenth. But on the Friday morning he'd set a new lap record and was heaps quicker than Melandri. I knew I had to do something so I laid out all the time sheets from every session that season on a table. I got Casey to come over and sit down and count everything up. It was ridiculous. At the majority of races he'd finished at least one session in the top two or three – all around the world, at circuits he had never been to before. I said, "Mate, just keep doing what you're doing and one day this is all going to translate into wins. It's just experience! You're going to blow all of these guys into the weeds." He was ready to pack it all in right there and then. It's very hard to get a kid through that, to keep their motivation up when they're not getting results. Unless the kid becomes complacent. Then it's easy because they don't care. They're happy just swanning around the Grand Prix paddock. Kids like that last a couple of years and then they disappear. I've seen them all come and go, in their big sunglasses, with their spiky hair and all the gear. They might be thinking, Well I'm struggling but at least I'm here, I'm a Grand Prix rider! They move on and the next crop of kids come through and the same thing happens again. Then you'll get a special kid who comes through and he'll stay.'

I wanted to be a stayer but for the first time I wasn't sure I could.

———— ———— ————

No matter how bad things were for me that year, they were even worse for Chaz. The owner of the team he was with hadn't really wanted him from the start, which set him up in an impossible situation. Chaz was growing into a tall kid and was already at a disadvantage on the smaller bike let alone getting screwed over by his team, which happened a lot because they didn't want to 'waste' any of their resources on him. Even though we tried to support each other it was difficult because we were both under pressure, a lot of it from the people who had given us these opportunities and couldn't understand why we didn't seem to be making the most of them. I think both of us would have been able to show our potential much sooner had we been in fully supportive teams from the outset.

Chaz Davies: 'It was tough … I remember a lot of times Colin looking around and saying to my dad, "It's bloody hard here, this place is hard!" But there were a lot more expletives than that! We did quite a lot together in those first few years because, as I said before, it's not cheap to travel around the world and you do what you can to save money. We ended up staying together, travelling together quite a lot and sharing a lot of experiences. It was a tough time but I've also got a lot of good memories of being together with my dad, Colin and Casey back then.'

We did have some great times, though others may not have appreciated some of what we got up to. At the European tracks everyone uses motorised scooters to get around. At one particular track we could see people parking their scooters outside the toilets so Chaz and I decided to play a prank that we'd picked up from a few of the older GP riders. While the scooter owners were inside Chaz and I gaffer-taped the horn button of their bikes so the horn stayed on. They'd come out of the amenities block, put the key in the ignition and start the engine. As soon as they did, the horn would start screeching so they'd turn it off, then try again. It would take them a while to work out what was going on. We were out of sight, watching. We thought it was hilarious but it was one of those jokes that you can only play once or twice before word spread to watch out.

There were other fun moments but the bottom line was that we were there to race. It was a steep learning curve, maybe too steep, but perhaps if it hadn't been that way I wouldn't have had the opportunity to get on a competitive 125cc in 2003. Despite all my problems with Massimo Biagini that season, Lucio Cecchinello and I had a good relationship. He was always supportive throughout the season despite my results not being as good as I'd have liked and he proved this with an offer to be his teammate in the smaller class for my second year. He confirmed we'd have a different crew chief, Massimo Branchini, and a new data engineer, Cristian Gabbarini, who by pure coincidence would later become my crew chief at Ducati. Otherwise it was largely the same team, including Chris Richardson, a mechanic from Northern Ireland who I trusted a lot and who became a firm friend.

Cristian Gabbarini: 'My job was to do data analysis with Casey in 125cc and analysis has no feelings, just numbers. The numbers said from the beginning he was really fast, he knows how to ride the bike really well, he knows where to put the tyres, but he was a little bit lost. It was his second year in Grand Prix but his first year in 125cc so it was something new again, but he was really sure of himself. He had a steel heart. If he believed in something he really pushed hard.'

The last 125cc I had ridden was a kit Honda in the Spanish Championship so the Aprilia was a lot different and it was difficult to get used to at the start of the season after losing some of my confidence on the 250cc. The main positive was that I could talk to my crew chief and he'd listen to what I had to say. He was gentle and quiet and very good to work with. Branchini spent a lot of time with me and because of him I started to learn how to communicate properly with a team of mechanics. I learnt what they needed to know in terms of what was wrong with the bike, where I needed it to be better. My ability to do that all started from him. I think it was mainly a confidence thing and he listened to me because he wanted to know, whereas Massimo Biagini never wanted to know what I thought or didn't care. It made such a difference being asked the right questions and that got me working in the right way. I was still young, I needed to learn and he was the perfect person for me to learn from.

I also picked up a lot from Lucio, who took me under his wing and helped me out at many different circuits when I was struggling. Because we were on the same bike, Lucio would come out with me for a few laps and show me around the track, so I could understand where I was losing time. He also taught me how to read telemetry (a data-gathering computer system that shows you where you are fast or slow compared to other riders), which in turn helped me to understand exactly what was happening out on the track. Things were looking up, or so I thought.

CHAPTER 7

A DIFFERENT TRACK

With the help of Lucio and Massimo Branchini any doubts about my ability that had started to niggle during the previous season disappeared and I could definitely see I was making progress as a rider. We still had some setbacks but I was now mixing it regularly with a talented group of riders at the front of the pack, including four guys who would continue to be huge rivals for the rest of my career: Dani Pedrosa, Jorge Lorenzo, Andrea Dovizioso and Marco Simoncelli. When you look at that list of names it's pretty amazing. The five of us were in there together right the way through our careers and if it wasn't for Marco's tragic death in 2011 we would have almost certainly been the top five championship finishers in MotoGP in 2011 and 2012. In my opinion we came through the toughest era in modern times because we were so competitive.

Hector Barbera was another strong young rider competing with us, as were Alvaro Bautista and Alex De Angelis, although for one reason or another they never managed to fulfil the potential they showed at the time. There were also experienced guys like Stefano Perugini, Roberto Locatelli and Steve Jenkner who also made life hard on the track that season.

There was some tough racing and at times I lost out in the frenzy of ten guys going for the same piece of track on the final lap. Jorge Lorenzo, in particular, was unpredictable to ride against in the early days and I wasn't a fan of his back then. There was no doubt he was fast but, by his own admission, he was extremely arrogant and a very cocky young kid. He'd tell you himself he thought too much of himself and his antics on the bike were often verging on dangerous. De Angelis, or 'Alex Dangerous' as Chaz and I used to call him, was another unpredictable rider, although his tactics were often more intentional. He'd already shown me one of them at Donington.

The 2003 season started out with a crash at Suzuka but after taking some points in the next three rounds, including a fourth place at Le Mans, we gradually established ourselves as a podium threat and in the fifth round of the season at Mugello I set my first pole position, only to get taken out in the final lap of the race by Steve Jenkner. After crashing out of the lead group again at Barcelona I was chasing Jenkner for the win in wet conditions at Assen but Dovi's bike missed a gear and I hit his back wheel and ended up in the gravel trap. I had to lay the bike down before I hit a wall. (That crash would affect more than one race; the back injury I sustained would go on to plague my career.) It was frustrating because I knew I had the potential to have been on the podium in each of those races but the most important thing was that with Branchini's help I was able to understand the crashes and turn those negative experiences into a positive by learning from them.

At Sachsenring in Germany it all finally paid off and I scored my first Grand Prix podium with a second place after fighting for the win until the last corner with Perugini and De Angelis. I probably had the speed to win that race but one part of the track was letting me down. Sachsenring is a tight circuit but it has some fast sections on a 125 and I wasn't riding them hard enough – I was too nervous. Anyway, the important thing was that we achieved a podium, which was a huge relief. The funniest moment in all that was the way Mum reacted. She'd been watching the race on the circuit television from our motorhome (you could tap into the signal and watch all the action that was being screened into the pit boxes). During the last two laps she couldn't stand the suspense so she turned her back. Chaz's parents were there and shouted out, 'Casey's second, he's on the podium.' That was it, Mum took off in her heels and had to run across the paddock, down some stairs, through the tunnel under the track, back up more stairs (discarding the heels because they were slowing her down), along the back of the pit boxes, then defy a young security guard and try to fight her way to me through the crowd at parc fermé, the secure area where the bikes are parked post-race. She wasn't going to miss my first podium win in Grand Prix. It had been a long time coming.

That good feeling didn't last long, unfortunately. In the next round at Brno, in the Czech Republic, I was trying a new experimental chassis for Aprilia (it used to buck so hard we called it 'Chainsaw' after a famous Australian rodeo bull). I'd finished fourth fastest in the wet in morning free practice and was running second fastest after six laps of first qualifying in the dry when it spat me off and I hurt myself pretty badly, breaking my collarbone and scaphoid.

A broken collarbone is a fairly common injury for a racer and not too serious because they normally heal okay, but the scaphoid is bad news, even though it is a tiny little bone, no bigger than a cashew nut. First of all, it is in an extremely important part of the wrist, just below the thumb, where you need a lot of strength, stability and flexibility. Secondly, it has limited blood circulation to it so it is a bone that doesn't heal well and if it is not fixed quickly and properly it will die. Together with the doctors at the Clinica Mobile (the medical clinic that travels with every race) the team organised for us to head straight back to San Marino for surgery to staple the bone back together and my wrist was fitted with a small cast.

The surgeons insisted the operation had been a success

but I should have known something wasn't right because the pain afterwards was incredible. Dad had to give me daily injections of pain relief and the wrist was badly swollen. I had three weeks to recuperate until the next race in Portugal and after a fitness test that consisted of me doing push-ups to prove I could ride, I got out on the track with nothing but heavy strapping on the wrist.

The collarbone had healed pretty well and the wrist didn't actually hold me back too much on the bike. In fact, I was the fastest rider on track and sat in provisional pole position until the engine seized on me during qualifying. Normally I'm quick enough to grab the clutch before the rear wheel locks up but because my wrist was not 100 per cent and strapped up I couldn't reach the lever fast enough. The bike threw me over the top and my collarbone broke where it had broken before.

Even though everything still wasn't perfectly healed I managed to get on the podium two weeks later in Brazil after a good battle with Lorenzo and De Angelis. I'd tried to lead on a few occasions that season and got messed up at the end so in this race I took my time and felt I had positioned myself perfectly for the last lap. I knew I didn't have the speed to slipstream more than one person down the long back straight there so I got myself into second place behind De Angelis and lined him up. Unfortunately that made a big hole in the air for Jorge, who was riding well and had a massive power advantage over us on the straights. He came past both of us and I couldn't get him back in the few corners left. I had done everything I could, so to not finish the job off was really disappointing.

It happened again in Japan in a race Dani Pedrosa was looking sure to win until he had a problem with his steering damper, which opened it up to the rest of us. I got in a fight with Hector Barbera and I was faster than him around most of the track but couldn't make anything stick because he was so late on the brakes. I remember that weekend we were running a new rear brake disc that had been provided by one of the team's sponsors. I like to use a lot of rear brake and during warm-up at Motegi, my bike locked up. I thought it had seized but what had actually happened was that the disc had got too hot, warped and locked the rear wheel.

The following weekend we went to Malaysia and I was having a good race, coming from eighth on the first lap to chase Dani for the lead. After about six laps the engine seized on me going into turn one and I immediately thought, That's my race over. I grabbed the clutch and then let it out to see if it would keep going, which luckily it did. I'd dropped back to sixth place and lost contact with the lead group but I decided to carry on and look out for it happening again. The bike started running faster than it had all weekend, which is normally a sign that the engine is about to blow up, so I quickly caught right back up and gave myself a great chance of winning the race. Once I had riders in front of me I couldn't get on the gas where I wanted to and had to be a bit more smooth. A lap or two later I was opening the throttle nice and gently when it seized again and threw me over the top. I badly bruised my hands and the fingers on my right hand were completely black. I had to race at Phillip Island the next weekend so I had to try and reduce the swelling as quickly as possible. Dad helped me hold my hands in ice water straight after the crash. I don't think I have ever experienced pain like that. But it worked!

Australia was next and after qualifying on the front row in the dry I was leading for the first five laps in the wet, with me and Stefano Perugini breaking clear of the rest of the field. With so many long, fast corners at Phillip Island, throttle control is key and I assisted it by using the rear brake a lot. We were still using the disc brake that had let me down in Motegi and as I went into Lukey Heights, the highest point of the Phillip Island circuit at turn nine, the rear locked up and came round on me like it had seized again. At first I thought it was my mistake and I was prepared to cop it but as soon as I picked up the bike and looked at the brake I realised it wasn't.

After Phillip Island, we went back to Europe for the final round of the season at Valencia with a new plan. I'd worked out that spending every lap at the front didn't work, playing games behind didn't work for me either and sometimes I'd missed out on the opportunity to attack. Because Valencia wasn't a big slipstreaming circuit we decided we had to be at the front on the last lap and just try to finish it off. I went to the front on the second lap and even though Simoncelli ran with us for a while there was only Hector Barbera who could consistently keep my pace. He and I swapped places a few times but I managed to make sure I was in front for the final lap, covered our lines and braked extremely late to cancel out his main strength.

Hector's only option was to try and come around the outside in the very last corner, a long left-hander, but there was no way he was going to make the turn and he ran off track, so the win looked certain to be mine. Then, just as I got on the gas to come into the final straight my spark plug broke and instead of revving to around 15,000rpm the engine maxed out at 11,000rpm. On a 125cc, which has a very short power range, that doesn't feel good. I kept expecting everybody to start flying past me before we hit the chequered flag. I was tucked in as hard as I could under the fairing, praying not for the win but that I would at least make it to the line!

Thankfully the gap we had built at the front was just big enough so that nobody could take advantage and I was able to celebrate my first ever Grand Prix win at the end of my second full season. Standing on the podium, listening to the Australian national anthem for the first time since my last win in the Spanish Championship at Jerez in November 2001, was a moment of pure relief. I was happy that Dad, James Strong and his wife, Jeanne-Claude, were there to see me win but Mum was back home in Australia watching on television. She immediately called Dad and insisted he put me on the phone so she could congratulate me despite everyone wanting me up on the podium. Finally, MotoGP journalist Gavin Emmett, who was commentating the televised race broadcast said over the air, 'Could someone take the phone off Bronwyn!' I don't think Mum was listening to the TV by then but I eventually said goodbye and made it to the presentation. Standing there, I thought about everything we had been through, the work we had put in, the opportunities that had passed us by; the bad luck and the mistakes. Finally, it had all been worth it and we could go back to Australia at the end of that season with some good options on the table for 2004.

From a financial point of view we were struggling again and the only money I had been able to bring in during 2003 was spent on getting us to the next race. Thankfully we were given some help from unexpected sources, one of which was an Australian businessman, Rod Lamb, and his wife, Carolyn, who were big MotoGP fans. They'd been travelling around Europe coming to some races and they approached us in Italy, surprising us with an offer of a chunk of money to help us out. After spending the weekend with us they'd seen how we were living and how hard and stressful it was and they doubled their offer. It was incredibly generous and there was nothing in it for them, they just wanted to help and we were extremely grateful. They have stayed good friends of the whole family.

Another person who helped us out massively was James Strong. When it came to motorcycle racing James was primarily a fan but he also became involved with Dorna,

MotoGP's TV and commercial rights holder, at board level and, as I mentioned earlier, over the years he took a direct involvement in my career, advising us on contract negotiations and introducing us to important sponsors. On one occasion he dipped into his own pocket to give us some money which helped us to fly back to Australia during the off-season, when we really couldn't afford to. I even had enough to buy my first (second-hand) ute, which I still have to this day. But, above all, James was a good friend and I was looking forward to spending more time with him in his new role as chairman of V8 Supercars. Sadly, he became critically ill following routine surgery in early 2013. His death shortly afterwards was a huge blow, to me personally but also to Australian motorsport and business in general and he will be greatly missed.

With James's generous help we were considering three offers for 2004: stay with Lucio on basically the same technical and financial package as 2003, move to the Scot Honda team to replace Andrea Dovizioso on what was basically a factory Honda or take a risk and sign for KTM, a factory team but with just one year's experience in Grand Prix and no results to speak of. Our first choice was Scot Honda but it turned out their offer was just a ploy to force Dovi into signing; I guess he was holding out for more money or something. We were hanging on, waiting for them to draw the contracts up on the assumption the deal was done but we never heard anything back and then Dovi signed. That's the way of the paddock, there is a lot of business like that happening.

Thankfully the offer from KTM was still open, which was a good thing because Mum and Dad had had to sell the house they had been renting out in Australia just so we could get back to Europe for the new season. We were now completely out of any savings and had nothing to fall back on. Signing with KTM meant drawing a decent wage and, in splitting from Lucio, we would also be free to do a deal directly with Spidi for my leathers. For the first time since leaving Australia we thought we would actually break even. That was a very proud moment for us and we happily signed.

From a technical point of view it was a risk to leave what we knew was a good package, even though it was in a private team, to take a factory ride on an unproven machine. KTM had come into the championship the previous season and signed two World Champions with Arnaud Vincent and Roberto Locatelli but their results hadn't been so good. On the positive side we would have an entire factory behind us, a very good engine tuner in Harald Bartol and the opportunity to work with an experienced and successful crew chief in Australian ex-racer Warren Willing, who had won the 500cc title just four years previously with Kenny Roberts Jr.

The KTM money also allowed us to buy a twin-axle enclosed trailer, which we got from Mario, and a car, a white Fiat Cinquecento that Chaz and I christened 'The Baked Bean' because it was so small we could put it in the trailer and tow it around Europe on the back of the Spidi motorhome. Dad built what he jokingly called fold-out bunk beds into the trailer but in reality they were three bits of 6×2 pine sheets that we set up each time we wanted to use them. When we arrived at a circuit we'd unload the car and convert it into extra sleeping quarters for me and Chaz, whose parents would join my mum and dad in the motorhome.

There was no air-conditioning or windows in the trailer so we slept with the doors wide open and a fan going at each end to circulate the air. There was always a smell of oil and petrol inside from carrying the Baked Bean around but after a Grand Prix weekend in the heat of the European summer with two teenage boys on board, the air got pretty bad! Gavin Emmett nicknamed the trailer 'the hamster cage' because it was so cramped but really we didn't care. The only time it bothered us was when, because it wasn't a proper motorhome, race officials kept trying to make us park it outside the paddock, in one of the car parks where there was no power. When we did have electricity we'd hook up the PlayStation and have some fun.

That season we were on our way from Barcelona up to Mugello when the axle snapped on the motorhome. We had to get towed from the highway and it ended up costing us €3500 to travel 5 kilometres. We got to a garage in a small town in Italy and started ringing around but nobody in Europe had an axle to suit it. We could have had one flown in from America but we were due at Mugello, so in the end Dad said, 'Let's weld it.' The Italian mechanics didn't think that was a good idea and kept saying, 'Impossible, impossible.' Dad kept replying, 'Possible, possible!' We went to an engineering shop and even they said you can't weld an axle. In the end Dad insisted so much they said they'd do it but that they didn't agree with it. He got them to put the axle on a lathe and taper the two broken ends down to nothing. Then he asked them to put the two points together and weld around it, put it back in the lathe and straighten it. They kept building it up, layer after layer, welding around the joint. This whole process took a couple of days so in the meantime Lucio's father came down and picked us up and towed the hamster cage to the circuit. Chaz and I slept in that and our parents got a hotel. The next week we picked up the motorhome and drove it back to Barcelona. We were thinking the whole way, I hope she's going to make it. But she was good as gold after that, and is still going to this day!

Thankfully the bike seemed to be more reliable than the motorhome and I took my second podium of the season that weekend at Mugello with a second place behind Locatelli, after taking third in the opening round in South Africa. We had a really fast engine from the start of the season and even though the frame wasn't the best I learnt to ride around the bike's problems. It must have been frustrating for Warren Willing, the crew chief, to have such a strong-minded young rider. My experience was starting to increase, and I was needing fewer laps to understand the bike. Warren was a good guy and he'd listen. At one race I pushed it but I got my way, they turned the bike upside down and I went 2 seconds quicker.

I had my first real chance to win in round six, at Assen, but I got screwed up by Jorge Lorenzo's antics on the final lap. The two of us were in a scrap with Locatelli and Dovizioso and I was the strongest in the last part of the track so I felt like I had the race under control. Lorenzo was on the grass in a few places, doing whatever he felt was necessary to make a pass, and midway around the final lap as we tipped into a flat-out left he came through and nearly wiped me out, costing me a couple of positions and, to my mind, potentially the win.

. It was typical of him at the time and I wasn't too happy but at least I felt like we were starting to make some progress with the bike, turning it into a genuine title contender. After another podium in Brazil we went to Germany trailing Dovizioso by just twenty-one points at the top of the championship. All we needed was that first win to really break through and having scored my first podium at Sachsenring the previous year I was confident this could be the one. Unfortunately, whilst setting the pace in free practice on the Saturday morning I crashed and broke my collarbone for a third time.

With only a week until the next race at Donington we decided to sit it out and came back at Brno after the summer break trailing Dovi by fifty-nine points at the top of the championship but still with seven races to pull it back. I lost the front on lap two and with Dovi finishing second that pretty much ruled us out of the championship. I'm not sure about the level of input from the factory after we were no longer in the running. We definitely started to lose power and our top speed dropped. There was a lot of potential in that bike so it was a shame that just as we got the chassis sorted out we started to have issues with the engine.

We managed to ride around some of our problems and picked up some good results before the season was over, including my second career win at Sepang in Malaysia. It was KTM's first World Championship victory in road racing, and I was proud to have played my part.

——— —— ——

In 2004 my attitude had definitely changed and I was becoming more sure of my own opinion and abilities and as a result of that Dad and I were starting to disagree more often. I wanted to make more of my own decisions without his input and our relationship was starting to suffer as a result. It is probably a normal part of growing up but it was magnified because we were working together, living together and he was acting as my manager. As far as I was concerned he hadn't raced in a long time and had never ridden Grand Prix so really he had no idea of what it took, which generated a lot of friction between us. I tried to talk to him but we couldn't discuss anything without getting angry at each other.

In the past we might have disagreed over things to do with the bike but that would be about it. I knew my place and I respected Mum and Dad's decisions. But I was growing older and like any nineteen-year-old I was forming my own ideas. Things reached a tipping point at Phillip Island. There was a lot of expectation on me after the win in Malaysia, a lot of demands on my time, we were all under a bit of stress and no one reacted well. Things with Dad came to a head in the riders' box at Phillip Island. We ended up scuffling, which wasn't pretty for anybody.

Even with all that going on I still placed third in the race. It was a tough decision to tell my dad I wanted to do this on my own from then on. I'd already had some conversations with former racer Randy Mamola and a business colleague of his, Bob Moore, who worked for a big American management company called WMG, and I'd decided that the best thing for my career was to go with them.

Dad told me to do what I wanted but he wasn't going anywhere until he'd checked out the management contract. He said, 'Once I'm happy with the contract, you go for your life.' It annoyed me that he kept the negotiation going for weeks, knocking back this and knocking back that to the point where they just said, 'Yep, okay that's fine.' I didn't know at the time but he'd written a clause into the contract which allowed me to walk away whenever I wanted.

Mum and Dad moved back to Australia to their farm called the Shamrock, way out in the scrub about one and a half hours

from Tamworth. I didn't see them again for a few months.
They gave me what I wanted: space. Having spent almost
every waking hour with my parents for the previous nineteen
years it was a huge change for me to finally be on my own.
I moved into a tiny apartment near Lucio in Monaco, which
would help me save on a lot of travel costs, and for the first
time in all the years I'd been racing I had some money in my
pocket that I could do what I wanted with. It wasn't much, but
up to that point I hadn't seen a single penny of my earnings
and I suppose I resented that, even though in reality it was all
going back into my racing.

World Superbike Champion Troy Bayliss, a fellow
Australian, was living in Monaco at the same time and he was
very kind to me. I remember the first day I moved into my
apartment and the power wasn't due to be connected for a
couple of days, so Troy said I could go and stay with him and
his family until I got myself sorted out. He did lots of little
things for me while I lived there, like lending me a pushbike
to get me started cycling, and it was handy to have him around
to call on if I needed help.

Career-wise, we'd already done a deal with Lucio to go
back with him for 2005 on a semi-factory 250cc Aprilia, which
was similar to the bike I'd ridden in 2002 but now I had much
more experience and the benefit of hindsight to help me do
better. KTM also had a 250cc project on the go by then but
they wanted me to stay on the 125cc and I was ready to go
back to 250cc so I was keen to move on.

Like in 2002, we were one or two steps back from the factory Aprilias but we started off the season with some really good results, including my first 250cc wins in China and Portugal, which gave me the championship lead. After that Dani Pedrosa found his stride and won five of the next seven races and pulled a heap of points on us.

Not everything was perfect for us but we came back strong with a handful of podiums and a couple more wins in Malaysia and Qatar to give ourselves an outside chance of winning the championship when we went to Phillip Island with three rounds remaining. We knew that to keep our chances alive we had to win, second wasn't good enough, so after qualifying on pole position I pushed hard from the start. After three laps I had opened almost a second over the rest of the field but I got a bit over-confident, tried to keep the bike tight to one of the corners and the rear stepped out, sending me spinning to the ground. I was disappointed but it was always going to be very difficult to challenge Dani on a privateer Aprilia when he was on a factory Honda. The ultimate aim is to be a factory rider with the full support of a factory team. But getting to that point means working for it. To secure a ride you may only be offered a privateer team (who lease or buy a factory bike but don't have further support for the ongoing adjustments to a bike). There are different levels of private teams, good and bad. You want a good one!

It is tough when you know your rival is on a better package than you. Sometimes you can't help looking at somebody's bike when they are doing well and wonder if it really is better, or if it's you that needs to improve. But I never wanted to be the person pointing at somebody else's bike instead of focusing on what I had and over the years I think that was another thing that probably helped me to ride difficult bikes fast. I am always proud to be on whatever bike I'm on and even if it's not the fastest I love wringing its neck to push it as hard as it will go. When you win and you know your bike is not the best it means something extra.

It's fair to say that in 2005 I sometimes had to ride above the bike's comfort zone just to keep up with Dani, whereas he was riding within his limits a lot of the time. It's impossible to know for sure but I believe this experience prepared me better for MotoGP and improved me as a rider. With guys like Jorge Lorenzo and Andrea Dovizioso out there too, I had to ride to my limit every weekend. There was no opportunity to relax, no easy wins to be had. Every one of us had to take risks to win, but that's what we were all there to do.

The most important thing I had to learn was to keep my emotions under control. In racing it is important to make logical decisions rather than passionate ones. Some riders become too aggressive when they let emotion affect their decision-making process and as soon as you do that you are not in control anymore. Very rarely it happens to me and if it does I try and fix it quickly. I had to learn to do the same thing off the track. There were times, like when we were negotiating the Scot Honda ride at the start of 2004, when I felt like I'd built a connection with someone, got excited about riding their bike, only for them to pull the rug out from under me. I had to learn not to let those things affect me but over the years the small let-downs and half-truths change you and you can't help becoming more cynical.

I was definitely maturing, learning from my experiences and at the end of that year I had a look at the relationship with Bob and Randy. It hadn't worked out the way I thought it would. They had tried to advise me on everything from training to psychology without me wanting their input on these things and yet they hadn't brought us a single sponsor and were trying to cut in on deals that we already had. I didn't like that at all. The turning point was when they wanted me to switch from Nolan to a different helmet company because they offered more money. That wasn't what I wanted. I had a good relationship with Nolan and I felt I owed them because they'd supported me at the beginning of my career when no one else would. Those loyalties mean nothing to a management company; they just want to take their percentage. It was a big lesson and I decided to end our relationship. I knew I couldn't manage myself but I wanted someone who'd respect my opinions and loyalties. I decided to talk to Dad about it. We'd needed the space to change the way we worked together but once we set boundaries we both knew we could make it work. Dad stopped being part of my career other than on the management side from that point on.

Dad says now: 'Most fathers and sons have to work out how

to interact at various stages in their relationship. I had to learn that Casey was growing up and needed to make his own way and that was complicated by being under so much pressure and me trying to act as a father *and* as a manager.'

We worked it out and we have been working together ever since.

———— —— ——

Even though I didn't manage to bring home the title that year the important thing was that I'd shown my ability and potential. We had the option to stay with Lucio for another season and try again in 2006 but smaller category titles were not going to get me where I wanted to go. The smaller classes are a big deal in Spain and Italy and their former World Champions are seen as legends. But in America, Australia and the UK we don't care about them as much. It's all about winning the big one. It's where the hardest bikes to ride are and the best riders compete.

That is not to devalue the achievements of my rivals in those smaller classes because I tried everything to win those championships and they came out on top. But the goal for me was always to win in MotoGP and I wanted to get there as quickly as possible, whatever the route. Lucio had similar ambitions for his team and was trying to get something happening with Yamaha, which was an option we were keen on.

Ducati, who had a contract with Bridgestone tyres, were also interested but they cooled. We didn't just want to go to MotoGP, we were aiming to win a championship. With Valentino Rossi on Michelins we figured the only way to compete with him was to make sure we were on Michelins too. If we could get on the same bike then so much the better. In the end we reached an agreement with Yamaha, which would see me spend my rookie season on a satellite bike (which might be older than the prototypes of the factory riders) and then move into the factory team in the second year. It was the perfect deal and I couldn't wait to sign it and get started.

CHAPTER 8

CRASH TEST DUMMY

The end of the 2005 season could have had the Rolling Stones song 'You Can't Always Get What You Want' as its soundtrack. By then, in my mind I thought my MotoGP future was going to be with Yamaha but at the last minute they pulled back. I can't tell you why exactly because nobody ever told me.

Dad will tell you: 'We got pretty close [to signing a deal]. Lucio and I were negotiating for Yamaha to give us a bike or at least a discount on a bike. We thought it was going to happen and then we got down to the last meeting with the Japanese and they said no. We were like, "What now?"'

James Strong summed it up best: 'Each new season has its beginnings even before the end of the previous one. There is

141

a frenzied period of preparations, with intense negotiations to form teams, arrange sponsorships, testing and re-testing of new equipment, and modifications to existing machines throughout November, December, January and February, trying out tyres for lap after lap, testing at different racetracks around the world, with all riders and teams both new and experienced trying to find the right combinations, the right set-ups for brakes, suspension, handling and performance.'

Once the deal with Yamaha disappeared, we had to come up with a new direction. We knew we couldn't afford to lease a Honda because it was going to be too expensive. Dad and Lucio didn't have the money or the sponsors to make that happen but then Honda told us that Sito Pons was keen to give me a test.

Sito, a former 250cc champion, had been running a very successful satellite Honda team for several years. They'd won a bunch of races with riders like Alex Barros, Loris Capirossi, Makoto Tamada and Max Biaggi. The timing was perfect and it was a good option for us to ride a competitive bike on Michelin tyres with an established team, so it looked like I was going to get what I needed. Just a few days after the end of the season at Valencia I was back there to test with Sito.

Much like when I had stepped up from the 125cc to the 250cc the previous year, the 990cc V5 just felt right for me. Even though it was a much bigger bike it felt lighter than the 250cc, it was more agile and had more power. Of course it had been my dream to ride the two-stroke NSR500cc like

Mick Doohan, which sadly would now never happen, but the RC211V was still an incredible machine. It was already in its fifth season of development and as well as winning two championships with Rossi in 2002 and 2003, a bunch of other guys had won races on it: Barros, Tamada and Biaggi and the likes of Sete Gibernau, Nicky Hayden, Tohru Ukawa and Marco Melandri. That told me what a great bike it was.

That first test was a lot of fun. I was given some pretty ordinary tyres by Michelin just so I could get used to the bike but I ended up fourth fastest, within six-tenths of a second of Nicky Hayden, who had just finished his third season with the factory team, and a tenth of a second quicker than Carlos Checa, who was also testing for Sito. The guy from Michelin said that with those tyres I shouldn't even have been within a second of the front guys so he promised to let me try the same grade of tyres that the other guys were using on the second day but unfortunately it was wet. We had another good test a few weeks later at Sepang and I was feeling confident that things were going to happen. As soon as that first test at Valencia was over Sito started talking contracts, and I think we'd even signed, but unbeknown to me things were unravelling badly for him behind the scenes.

Dad remembers: 'It was all dependent on Sito securing sponsorship from the Camel tobacco brand for another year. That's where the whole thing fell to bits in the end because he couldn't close the deal and guarantee the money to Honda, who were hanging on and hanging on. They had a certain date that they wouldn't go past and Sito couldn't get sponsorship lined up so the whole thing fell through.'

After the drama with Yamaha and now this with Sito it seemed like every time we were making a move up everything collapsed beneath us. It was hard not to get discouraged and think it was never going to happen. But there is always a way if you are determined enough and back yourself. It did seem we were right back where we'd started with Lucio. In November, Dad and Lucio had a meeting with Dorna CEO Carmelo Ezpeleta, who was keen to see me in MotoGP, and he told us that Dorna would guarantee the money to Honda on Lucio's behalf, giving us the breathing space we needed to find a sponsor.

We had two months until the next test at Sepang and by January it was all sorted. In theory it was a decent package. As a satellite team we would be a couple of steps behind the factory Repsol Hondas, not having the same tyres or equipment, but even though the title had been won for the previous couple of seasons by Yamaha we still knew we had a great bike. We also had the dominant tyre brand, Michelin, and Lucio had put a strong crew together. He inherited some of the more experienced members of Sito's team, including crew chief Ramon Forcada, who had worked with Alex Barros for many years. Along with Chris Richardson, my trusted mechanic from my 125cc and 250cc days, it was a good team.

During the off-season Dad worked hard to get some

sponsors lined up. He went to the Milan motor show for a couple of meetings, one of which was with Alberto Vergani, President of Nolan helmets. I was already grateful to Alberto for the support he had shown us when we first moved to Grand Prix back in 2002 and I'd had the opportunity to pay him back a couple of years later when we had some problems with our visors steaming up in the rain. Dani Pedrosa split with Nolan over the issue but I valued Alberto's support and we stayed, in spite of more lucrative offers. I think Alberto appreciated it. What he did next seemed to tell me just that. Even though we still had a year left on our contract with Nolan as a 250cc rider, he tore it up, literally, in front of Dad's eyes. 'Casey is a MotoGP rider now,' he said, and he doubled the money on the spot without any need for negotiation. That was a huge thing and made us realise that it was time for us to start making changes in other areas. We didn't start making demands, we started chasing the right sponsors, the ones we wanted and, as Nolan showed, loyalty pays off. After all the years of scrimping and saving to chase the dream of becoming a MotoGP rider, the moment looked like it was getting closer. As part of the negotiations with Lucio we insisted on dealing directly with a protective equipment supplier. We did a deal with Alpinestars, which was the start of another fantastic relationship and a sign that things were definitely looking up.

We took delivery of the 2006 bike in time for the test at Sepang and did something like 170 laps over three days, finding a base setting for the chassis and suspension. We went on to Phillip Island and had three good days there, closing the gap to the factory bikes, before heading back to Sepang in mid-February for another test. Unfortunately that one would last just thirteen laps for me. I went through turn one and two riding as I always did, but the change in direction seemed to tweak my shoulder. I'd soon find out that I'd damaged the rotator cuff ligaments that I'd torn in that crash with Brad and Jason back at Tamworth when I was ten years old.

That was it. I had to go back to Australia for surgery, ruling me out of the remainder of the pre-season. Some people might have been happy to leave a European winter to head home to an Australian summer but I wasn't at all. It was time and money I didn't want to waste. But there was one positive, and it was a big one!

I was going to be able to spend some more time with Adriana Tuchyna, a girl I had been seeing for almost a year. We'd first met at Phillip Island back in 2003. Adriana came to ask me for an autograph. It was one of those funny moments that I'll never forget because Adriana was asking for an autograph and her sister Dorothy and the people around were egging her on so she asked me to sign her stomach too. I couldn't say no! (Later, I would realise how out of character that was; Adri is a very modest person and would never normally do something so bold.) Then her sister came up to me and we started chatting. She told me Adriana would really like my mobile number and I asked for hers. Adri is an

Chaz and I have been friends since Mallory Park in 2000, nothing has changed since then.

© Ian Newton

Trying to keep the front down over the famous 'mountain' at Cadwell Park, August 2000. I was riding for Lloyds and that year became the Aprilia Superteen Champion.

Lining up on the grid at Donington in 2001. Dad is on the far right talking to a Honda talent scout.

At Jarama in May 2001 with Leon Camier (*left*) and Chaz Davies (*right*).

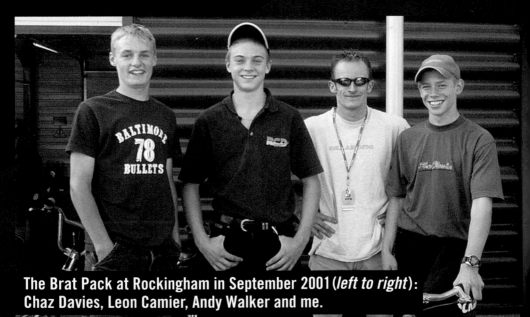

The Brat Pack at Rockingham in September 2001 (*left to right*): Chaz Davies, Leon Camier, Andy Walker and me.

Mum and Dad timing me as I came out of the first corner at Phillip Island. It was my first road race in Australia since we'd been forced to leave to chase the dream and so it was a huge moment for us all.

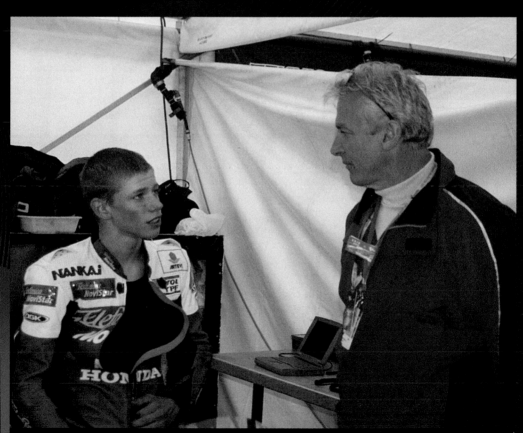

I wasn't just back home racing, I also got to meet one of my all-time heroes, motor racing legend Peter Brock. It gave me a real boost to have someone like him take an interest in me and give encouragement to a young bloke just starting out.

Standing on the podium in Valencia for my first win was a feeling of pure relief. I thought about everything we had been through up to this point – and it was all worth it.

The 2004 season was my first as part of a factory team. I learnt a lot from the crew at KTM. And my first win for that season, and the first ever for KTM, at Sepang (*right*) was awesome!

We gave all we had on the privateer Aprilia against the factory Honda but this crash when pushing for the win at Phillip Island ended our hopes for the 2005 championship. (*Left*): I met up with Adriana again in 2005, and here we are at our engagement party in 2006.

This was the motorhome we were living in, with what MotoGP broadcaster Gavin Emmett called 'the hamster cage' hooked up behind it.

© Andrew Northcott

© Andrew Northcott

© Andrew Northcott

In 2006, we had problems with the tyres all season and the year ended with an inexplicable front-end crash at Valencia. I started to doubt myself and my abilities. Without the support of my family and Adri it would have been really tough.

Ducati showed great faith in signing me up as a factory rider in 2007. Nobody could have predicted what we achieved together: winning ten races to clinch the title at Motegi with three rounds to spare. Valentino Rossi was quick to congratulate me in front of the cameras after my opening-round win in Qatar but as I continued to be a threat on the track his attitude changed throughout the years. I still respect him as a competitor.

Adri and I (pictured here with Mum and Dad) had planned our wedding in her hometown of Adelaide for 6 January 2007. She looked beautiful! But we didn't have time for a honeymoon because I had to get to Madonna di Campiglio for the Ducati team launch.

© Andrew Northcott

absolute stunner and even at fifteen turned heads. I'd noticed her walking around the paddock but I'd been too nervous to approach her so I was more than happy to get her number. There was something about Adriana I really liked. That night I texted her to ask if she'd be my umbrella girl for the race, I thought that might be something she'd think was fun. Over that weekend I spent time with her whole family and they were great people.

We lost contact for a while after that but then, in 2005, Adriana's brother, John, and Dorothy were racing in China during the MotoGP weekend and so we caught up. I had a great time hanging out with them both and they invited me to their place in Adelaide next time I was back in Australia. I won the race on the Sunday and there was a gap before the next one so I asked Lucio if I could fly to Adelaide the next day. It was perfect timing! Adriana didn't know I was coming and got quite a surprise when I turned up at the door. The first night we sat up talking for hours after everyone else had gone to bed. We really hit it off. By the time I left we were both keen to stay in touch and Jano and Vlasta, Adri's parents, gave permission for her to join me for the next few races in Europe. Up until that point I would spend time with the team when we were racing but apart from that I spent a lot of time on my own. It was wonderful to have someone outside of racing to talk to. And it's true, absence definitely makes the heart grow fonder. The more time I was away from Adriana the more I realised I wanted to be with her. We texted back and forth, emailed and phoned and it started to become more serious.

Adri flew over to see me before I had shoulder surgery at the beginning of the 2006 season in Sydney. It was six weeks before I was allowed to train so those weeks went by slowly. Adriana and I spoke often.

When I headed back overseas professionally things weren't looking so good. In those days there were no limits on testing so when I arrived in Europe for the first round of the season at Jerez I had missed nine days of testing; three in Malaysia, three in Barcelona and three at Jerez. It meant everybody was way ahead of us with their set-up and we struggled in practice at Jerez, especially when it came to adapting the bike to the softer qualifying tyres. We ended up finishing way back in fifteenth place out of nineteen riders on the grid.

James Strong puts it better than I can: 'A good start leading to a prominent position near the front of the field is very important. Being caught up in the back of the pack battling to pass bike after bike, trying to avoid being left too far behind the leaders is a big disadvantage. It saps energy, often causes excessive tyre wear, and slows even the fast riders as they are forced to take calculated risks to make their way up towards the leaders.

'So position on the grid is important to being able to start efficiently and try to get away cleanly. Racetracks always begin with a straight, which obviously varies in length from track to track, but all of the bikes arrive soon after a period of extreme acceleration from the start into turn one, usually in close formation, still jockeying for position.'

I made a great start off the line and our luck improved further in the first corner, when Toni Elías got his braking markers completely wrong, took out Valentino Rossi and opened up a gap for me to dive through. I was sixth by the end of the first lap and up to fourth two laps later, just behind Nicky Hayden in third. We'd changed the front forks after qualifying and the bike felt much better but I was running wide in some corners so I couldn't quite hang on to Nicky, eventually dropping back to sixth, but it was a massive boost to me to see that I could run with the lead group when things were working. It was just the boost I needed.

Adriana had flown over to Europe with her parents and was there for the Jerez race. After that we headed to Slovakia together. Adri's mum and dad are originally from Slovakia and still have a lot of family there, so we planned to spend a week with them staying with Adri's relatives. It didn't turn out quite as we'd planned because I got sick, really sick. I had cold sweats and a terrible fever, to the point where I couldn't walk and could hardly talk or even hear because my ears were blocked up. I was starting to improve when we made the short drive over the Austrian border for me to catch a flight from Vienna to Doha, Qatar, for the second race of the season. I had to say goodbye to Adri as she was going home to Adelaide.

When we arrived in Vienna we found out our flight had been delayed for 24 hours, so we ended up driving back to Adri's family's place until the next day. When we did eventually get a flight, for some bizarre reason the woman at the check-in put my tickets together with some guy who was travelling in business class who I didn't know. I didn't worry too much about it then but when I went to transfer to our connecting flight in Dubai they wouldn't let me board the plane until this guy turned up, even though my name was on the list. I waited for everybody to board and of course the guy didn't show. He must have taken an earlier flight but I had no way of knowing for sure. I was furious! I had to go all the way out of the terminal and book another flight but there wasn't an available seat until the next day. I didn't have a credit card back then so that made things a lot more difficult too. I spent 24 hours in Dubai airport and arrived in Doha 48 hours later than planned, with only an hour to spare before the first free practice was due to start.

I spoke to Lucio when I landed and he said, 'If your bags don't arrive within five minutes just leave them.' I arrived at the track ten minutes before the session started, got changed, got on the bike and set the fastest time of the session. I was four-tenths of a second inside the circuit record and two-tenths of a second quicker than my closest challenger, who was Valentino Rossi. I ran second fastest in the second session that afternoon, fastest in the third free practice the next morning and then qualified on pole position. I was the second youngest rider ever to do that after Grand Prix legend Freddie Spencer.

I suppose it was a bit too much to ask for that momentum to continue through the race. Since 2008 we have ridden at night in Qatar because the organisers wanted to introduce a night race into the calendar. Qatar was always a good race for us because of the hot conditions, the tyres would over-heat causing the bike to move around a lot more, and that suited me. I enjoyed racing in the heat but because of my lack of sleep and the hectic flight my sickness started to get worse again. I wasn't able to recuperate so by race day I was already worn out. I managed to hold off Rossi and lead for the opening nine laps of the race but I was tired so wasn't able to be as aggressive on the bike as I needed to be and I gradually dropped out of the podium positions and finished fifth, which was still a good result considering the lead-up. I wanted better though.

The next round was in Turkey and I was pretty much back to full fitness. It was only the second time the championship had visited the new circuit in Istanbul, which was an advantage to me because I learn tracks faster than other riders. I was second fastest after the first day of free practice in the dry but we had a lot of trouble with the Michelins in the wet on day two and even though I could only qualify seventh fastest Nicky Hayden was the only non-Bridgestone rider ahead of me on the grid.

Thankfully the weather improved for the race and the Bridgestone guys gradually went backwards, allowing me,

Nicky, Marco Melandri and Dani Pedrosa to come through and fight for the win. For a few laps it was like a 125cc race, the four of us constantly passing each other. I felt we had a faster pace than the guys in front so with five laps to go I went to the front of the pack to take the lead and try to pull a gap. Marco was able to up his pace and keep up. It was my first chance of a podium in MotoGP so I didn't want to risk too much that race and Marco was able to risk more. There was a long back straight at Istanbul, which was followed by a run of tight corners to finish the lap. Whoever was in front at the end of that back straight was going to win but I covered as much as I wanted to risk into that tight corner. Maybe I could have covered more but as I've said, I didn't want to throw away my first chance of a podium and I didn't care about championship points. Marco passed me and went on to win the race.

I got back to parc fermé and considering it was the team's first podium I didn't expect to see them disappointed I didn't win the race. The fact that it was our first podium in MotoGP was overlooked. If you watch that same team now they celebrate for results nowhere near what we achieved. I couldn't help wishing they reacted more positively when I came second in only my third race. I guess they took that early success for granted and the fact that they've only had one podium since then made them realise it isn't easy to make it up there and they should celebrate those moments more.

I finished fifth again in China, which was another decent result. I'd actually run off the track halfway through the race and dropped down to eleventh so had managed to fight my way back and pass guys when the tyres were well past their best. The next round was at Le Mans.

There is definitely no such thing as easy on that first corner at the Le Mans track. You have to brake on a lean and then briefly get back on the gas again before standing up and braking hard into a tight chicane. To make it even more difficult the track was damp that day so I backed off a lot earlier than I normally would have done but I still lost the front. It was the corner where Alberto Puig had a horrific accident in 1995 that led to the race being removed from the MotoGP calendar for five years until changes were made to the track. For a brief second that thought flashed through my mind. Luckily I was able to sit up and ride it out.

We had some set-up problems in qualifying at Le Mans and I couldn't go any faster on the softer qualifying tyre than I had in free practice on race rubber, which left us down in eleventh place on the grid. I struggled to hit my braking markers with a full fuel tank early in the race and was lucky not to take Nicky Hayden out on the first lap, but by mid-race I had started pulling back positions and ended up winning a really tough battle with Nicky to take fourth place by a couple of tenths of a second. It was the third time in five races that we'd finished ahead of one, if not both, factory Honda riders. In a way we soon became the victim of our own success.

Michelin had started to realise that I could do the lap times, especially on used rubber, so they started using me as a guinea pig. They would put me on a certain set of tyres for free practice and I would be happy as anything, right on the pace. Then on race day they'd say, 'You can't use that tyre.' They'd insist on us using a different tyre and then we'd find out on the grid that Dani or Nicky or somebody else was on the tyre I was planning to race on. Contractually we were obliged to use whatever tyre they decided on.

It wasn't like it is now where each rider gets an identical tyre allocation to work with for the whole weekend. Back then it was a free-for-all. You gave your feedback to Michelin and they decided what tyre was best for each session. We had a bunch to work with in practice but for the race they made our choice for us. We never knew what we were getting but we'd be running one tyre number all weekend and then for the race it would have a different batch number. Half the time the front and rear tyres didn't even match up. I'd go from practice, when everything was working well, and then in the race I'd tip into a corner and the front would fold. Sometimes the rear would offer too much grip for the front. They had so many different combinations of profile and compound at that stage.

I kept pushing because I trusted them but there were some massive crashes which I thought were caused by the tyre combinations I was given at the last minute. The first big one was at Mugello, a fast lowside after nine laps when I was running in third place. Thankfully it looked worse than it was and the bike bore the brunt of the damage; I escaped with a sore neck. The same thing happened in the next round at Catalunya in Spain, when I managed to get the two holeshots (first to the first corner) from the third row of the grid after the race was stopped because of a pile-up in turn one. Exactly nine laps after the restart I sat comfortably in second behind Rossi when the front folded again.

Dad will tell you, 'As outsiders, we'd always watched GPs and heard about these so-called tyre wars but we never understood how political it all really is. Michelin could control the championship, and could practically decide who was going to win. For some, they'd fly tyres in from France overnight! Casey never had any tyres flown in, I know that for a fact. If he got a tyre in practice that was three- or four-tenths of a second quicker than everybody else – and you can look at the time sheets if you don't believe me because this is what happened – they'd usually take it off him and give it to another rider. Casey would go out in the race and nearly always it would be the front that folded on him.'

Dad was right. I started feeling like a crash test dummy and as the season progressed the situation got worse, to the point where I'd get angry and go off. I got a reputation as a spoilt brat. I am not making excuses but I was frustrated. Dad would come over to Europe to try to settle things down but the fact was I felt the tyres were causing me to crash. My confidence also took a hit and it took me back to the doubts I had in my first season of Grand Prix in 2002. I started to question myself a lot. Was it me or the bike? After a while I couldn't be sure. It was my debut season in MotoGP and I really didn't know what I was capable of. I'd proved I was competitive but the race results weren't showing what I knew I could do. It started to mess with my head and unfortunately it seemed that my crew chief Ramon Forcada didn't have a lot of faith in what I was capable of either. He knew there were problems with the tyres but as far as he was concerned that was just the way it was. That's probably why, when you look at Alex Barros's career as an example, he was fighting to win races one weekend and then struggling to be on the podium at the next. But I never wanted to be a rider who tickles around in tenth place because he can't get a feel for the front and doesn't understand why.

Like I had done my whole life I kept pushing and, of course, I kept crashing and I got slammed for it in the paddock and in the press, earning myself the nickname 'Rolling Stoner', which really bugged me. The pressure began to build as people questioned my talent and Ramon started to suggest that I was crashing because I wasn't physically fit enough. I knew this couldn't be the only solution, and I still couldn't work out why I kept crashing. As a rookie I wasn't to know any better but people around me with experience should have helped me to understand the tyre issue.

I would come in after a race saying, 'I didn't do anything wrong, I didn't make a mistake. I would know if I had.' But they would say, 'Well, you must have done because you crashed.' All the blame went to me and with everybody telling me it was my fault, I started to believe it. Ramon is a very good crew chief, extremely skilled at setting up a motorcycle, but I wish he'd listened to me a little more.

Probably the biggest thing I learnt from that season and the one before was not to trust people with more experience purely because of that experience. It would prove to be one of the most important lessons of my career. Often Dad and I would find ourselves looking up to people who we had only previously seen from the outside and we viewed them as having so much knowledge of the sport. I guess they liked that feeling and didn't need any encouragement to make us feel small and insignificant. We had no choice but to trust them and that could have ended my career before it had even started. By the end of that season I realised that nearly everyone has an agenda and it isn't always for you to win.

On the morning of the race at Sachsenring, Germany, in round ten, I crashed again during warm-up. It was another lowside and it happened at turn eleven, one of the fastest corners in the entire championship. When I got to my feet the marshals asked me how I was but I didn't answer immediately, I was biting my lip because of the intense pain in my fingers, which had just been dragged across the gravel at 200km/h, and I was too busy contemplating the fact I had just destroyed my bike with only a couple of hours to go before the race.

With my mind on other things I wasn't worried about myself, just the bike! When we got to the medical centre for a check-up the marshals reported my condition and said that the fact I hadn't immediately responded to them was a sure sign of concussion, as was the fact that my fingers were stinging. With the greatest respect to all the marshals around the world who volunteer their time to help us go racing, they are not qualified to make a call on the medical condition of a rider. Yet, for some reason, the circuit doctors took their word for it and declared me unfit to race.

I couldn't believe they were making such a drastic call when I didn't even have so much as a scratch on my helmet. Eventually they said I could race if I went to the hospital for a scan and it came back clear. To make that happen I had to be quick so we jumped in a helicopter and went and got a scan done, which obviously came back clear, but by the time we got back to the circuit the race officials had already confirmed the official starting grid without me being included. That was another huge let-down for me, and over the years I have seen huge inconsistencies in who they let race under certain circumstances and who they don't.

Was it all political that season? I can't tell you that but occasionally I thought so. I remember at Phillip Island we had a few problems with the bike but we got it sorted in warm-up and I set the fastest time of the session – we were flying. Then, just before the start of the race, Honda officials told us we couldn't use the gearbox setting we had because supposedly the fuel wouldn't make it to the end. Maybe they were right but to me it just seemed like Honda didn't like the idea that I might beat their factory bikes. There were lots of things happening like that, one after the other, which made me realise just how little control a privateer team has.

The only thing that stopped me from walking away from the sport right there and then was the fact that in the penultimate round of the season at Estoril in Portugal we signed a deal with Ducati to ride for them in 2007. For the first time in my life I would be on a factory bike and, perhaps more importantly considering my suspicion that tyres were a big factor in my lack of podium performances, we'd be on Bridgestone tyres. We had known about their interest for a while but we had also been in negotiations with the Yamaha factory. Around the same time James Strong was attending a Formula 1 race and he got talking to one of the Yamaha bosses, who told him that I'd been making demands for crazy amounts of money. None of that was true and James, being a very good friend and someone who had helped us with advice over the years, told us what was going on.

From what James passed on it became really clear to us that somebody inside Yamaha didn't want me there and they were obviously doing all they could to make sure the deal didn't happen. We didn't even challenge what they offered us and accepted their first proposal without issue. The only thing we insisted on was that we would be part of the same garage as Valentino Rossi and Jeremy Burgess so that we could learn from them. It was a factory team and we wanted to be fully a part of it so I didn't think that was an unfair request. This was the sticking point and even though we'd all agreed to the rest of the contract we could not get agreement on this simple issue.

With Yamaha a no-go, the only other option on the table was to stay with Lucio, on the same bike and deal as 2006. So we decided to give Ducati a go. To have a factory team showing such faith in me when I was starting to lose faith in myself meant a hell of a lot. I wanted nothing more than to get some podiums and maybe the victory that had eluded me that year in Turkey; to put every factory Honda and every factory Yamaha behind me just once and make them sorry that they passed me up. I didn't think I could win the championship straight away and I told Ducati this. But that didn't mean I wasn't going to try.

———————

After Adri and I had been together for a year I knew she was the one for me. I didn't want to waste any more time apart so I discussed with a couple of my friends and my dad how I felt. They all said the same thing: 'Mate, she's a great girl.' I think anybody who meets Adriana realises that she's a pretty special woman. Yes, she's beautiful but she's also caring, calm and extremely clever, way more than me. She also doesn't take any grief from my friends like Leon, Stork or Chaz, she just fits straight in and gives it back to them.

Adriana and I had talked about the future and I knew that she felt as strongly about our relationship as I did. I decided I was going to propose. This is what we both wanted but we hadn't made anything official or told anybody so after the race at Mugello I flew down to Adelaide to visit her. I'd bought a ring for Adri a month earlier, while Chaz was visiting me in Monaco. He'd come with me on a drive to Ventimiglia. Troy Bayliss had arranged for me to meet with a friend of his who was a jeweller down there. After asking her father's permission, Adriana's mum helped me organise a limousine to pick us up from their place. Adriana had no idea what was going to happen, but maybe she suspected when the limo turned up. I wanted to take her to dinner at a fancy restaurant in town, where I was going to do the full proposal but when Adri's mum had made the reservation for me they failed to tell her that part of the restaurant was closed for renovations. When we arrived they went to seat us next to their bar area with poker machines in the background. I didn't want to ask her there so after dinner we went for a walk in the park.

Adriana says now: 'It was really sweet and even though I was only seventeen I had no hesitation to say yes. I know it is pretty unusual for anyone our age to get engaged but I don't think my friends were too shocked when they found out the next day at school. I knew I wanted to spend my life with Casey and as far as I was concerned there was no reason for us to wait any longer. Some people have dreams of going to university, travelling or partying but my dream was to marry the person I love and have a family together. I feel very blessed that my dream has come true.'

———— ———— ————

Knowing that my future was with Adri made me want more than ever to chase success. But just because my private life was looking great didn't mean that my racing suddenly came together. That season finished with two more crashes in the last two races at Estoril, when ironically I took out the guy I would be replacing at Ducati, Sete Gibernau, and Valencia, taking my total number of crashes that season to fourteen. Apart from my fellow rookies Randy de Puniet (fourteen) and Dani Pedrosa (eight) no other rider had more than six crashes that season. Valentino Rossi had just three, the last of which came at Valencia and cost him the championship. When I saw it later on television, it looked strangely familiar.

The title had gone down to a final-race decider between Valentino and Nicky Hayden, with Valentino ahead by eight points. Basically Nicky needed the most unlikely possible scenario – a Rossi crash – to win a championship that he had led for most of the season until he was taken out by Dani at

Estoril. Valentino was in great form that weekend and had qualified on pole by a couple of tenths of a second, with Nicky fifth on the grid, so it looked like it was Valentino's race to lose.

But as soon as the lights went out Valentino was in trouble. I was one of six riders to pass him on the first lap and if you watch the footage you can see how much he is struggling to even keep up with us. His rear and front tyres were just not working together and on lap five the front inexplicably folded and he went down, right behind me. I couldn't help but wonder how he could be having such problems with his tyres. Could he really have been stitched up? It seemed so improbable, but I remember watching that race back in the motorhome that evening and thinking, Welcome to my world, mate.

CHAPTER 9

DREAMS COME TRUE

Things were changing and even though there was so much to be excited about, the publicity demands of being in a factory team were going to take some getting used to. Just like when I was a kid lined up for my first race at Hatcher's, it was the attention that I struggled with. Racing is the easy part, it is what I love; it's the interviews, the dinners, strangers wanting to know private details that I find hard. Which I know all sounds a bit odd complaining about when you are writing a book about your life, but I still struggle with that, too.

Adri and I had planned our wedding in her home town of Adelaide for 6 January 2007. Like most couples, we were nervous, excited but most of all really happy we were getting married. Yes, some people thought us too young but we knew what we wanted and weren't bothered by the opinions of others. We were looking forward to our honeymoon and spending time together without any other demands. That was the plan, but a few weeks before our wedding day Ducati told me I had to be in Italy the week after the wedding to be ready for the official team launch in Madonna di Campiglio. We had to give up the idea of a honeymoon and get ready for that.

On the day itself we had 150 guests and all eyes were on us. Adriana looked incredibly beautiful as she walked down the aisle of St Peter's Cathedral on her father's arm. My cousin Mark was my best man and standing there at the front of the church I almost couldn't believe I was marrying the girl of my dreams. I wanted that day to be wonderful for Adriana's sake, and it was. Somebody leaked the venue details to the press and we had photographers turning up and taking pictures, but we weren't going to let anything get us down. It went so fast and was all a blur but at the end of it all we were husband and wife so I couldn't have been happier.

The next day we had to be on a flight to Europe and before we even realised it we were on the plane. It was a whirlwind and we arrived in Italy to be met by television cameras and photographers following our every move. Compared to previous satellite teams, the PR side with Ducati was a lot more organised and controlled, so even though there was a lot more work, in a way it was more manageable. But I was suddenly under a lot of pressure to do the part of the job that I hated the most. I was now a factory rider, employed by probably the most prestigious motorcycle racing brand in Europe, and the Italians wanted to know everything about me and my new gorgeous wife.

The team launch, called 'Wrooom', is held with the Ferrari F1 Team. Together the two racing teams pretty much take over an entire ski resort in the Dolomite mountains, all paid for by the Philip Morris tobacco company, which sponsors both factories' racing activities. It is an extravagant affair with no expense spared and the bill must run into millions of dollars. The whole thing lasts a week, with press conferences in the morning followed by one-to-one interviews and then some 'spare time' in the afternoon to go skiing.

It's an incredible event and if I loved the spotlight it would be heaven but to have my every move captured by the cameras, even eating dinner in the evening, felt very uncomfortable for me. Having all that happen within the space of two weeks – the build-up to the wedding, the day itself, the flight to Europe and then a week under the spotlight as a factory MotoGP rider with the biggest sponsor in the championship – was a lot to take. I am afraid I didn't handle it perfectly because it was so new to me and it wasn't fair on Adri that the early days of our marriage were put under so much stress. The bright side was we were really good at talking things through together and going through that experience without Adri there would have been so much harder.

And let's be honest, this was part of what I had to do to be a rider in a factory team and have the bike, tyres and support to race well in MotoGP, which was what I had always wanted to do. Hopefully my days of unsuitable tyres were over! Joining a factory team might have meant joining a media circus but it also meant full support at the racetrack and Ducati were keen to create an environment where I was happy.

At my first test in Valencia I noticed a few of my mechanics didn't seem too thrilled to be working with me. The rumours around the paddock had labelled me a difficult rider to work with, plus I was branded as a crasher. They hadn't really met me before but by the end of the first day all that had changed and we had the start of a very strong team. I'm thankful to Team Principal Livio Suppo, who put together a crew of hard-working, highly motivated people, led by my new chief mechanic Cristian Gabbarini. I wasn't sure about having Cristian as my crew chief at first as it was a job he had never done before. Because I was relatively inexperienced I felt I needed somebody with more experience than me but it turned out to be a great decision. We were both like blank canvases ready for fresh ideas, so that when we arrived at a new track we weren't fixed in our ways about how the bike was supposed to be set up or ridden.

Cristian says: 'Casey already knew Italians and the Italian style and he felt really, really good with us from the beginning. When he wanted some quiet time, he came into the garage and asked me or Gabriele, the electronics guy, "May I sit here a bit at your table or play with my laptop with you guys? Because outside there are too many people." It was strange for him but he was like our younger brother. He helped us to change the team into a family. And for him that was really important I think.'

The other bonus about becoming a factory rider for the first time is that there was no extra pressure in terms of results. I had a more senior teammate in Loris Capirossi, who had won a bunch of races already, and the terms of my contract showed that Ducati weren't expecting too much too soon. Dad had negotiated a deal for a low base salary but big results-based bonuses, which gave me the opportunity to multiply my wages if I could pull off the unlikely and actually win a race here and there. In that respect the pressure was off but we were confident; confident that Ducati would produce a competitive bike to meet the new 800cc engine limit regulations, confident in the potential of the Bridgestone tyres and confident in my ability. What we couldn't have expected was just how perfectly all of those things would fit together, starting from the first day of winter testing at Valencia in Spain.

Cristian remembers: 'Again for him it was something completely new, because it was from five cylinder 1000cc to four cylinder 800cc and Bridgestone tyres instead of Michelin tyres. So I put the data at zero again. But he was in a good mood. Casey said, "I have to learn with this bike, you guys have to help me. Let me know if there is a certain way you need me to ride this bike, I can adapt." We worked together for two days which was really easy and in the end the result was really good. I think Casey finished with the second-best lap time, or something like this.'

To be honest, in that first test at Valencia the bike was savage, a real pig to ride and I thought, What have I done? I never let that affect me on the bike, though. It probably made me more determined to get things right. We went to Jerez at the end of December, just before the winter testing ban kicked in, and it wasn't much better. We did some work with the engine to smooth out the power delivery under acceleration and I finished just a tenth of a second behind Loris, who had won the race there earlier in the year. Even though we had a lot of problems to solve I went home for Christmas feeling happy. Finally I had people who believed in my talent, who were listening to me and reacting to what I was saying. When I saw that my feedback had a positive effect on the modifications made to the bike it gave me even more belief in myself and I started to trust my own opinion again, something I had lost in the 2006 season. It was nice to know.

We made good progress in the first test of 2007 at Sepang, where I got a real taste of just how good the Bridgestone tyres were. The stability I was getting from the front was like nothing I had ever had before and I set my best lap of the three-day test on a rear tyre that already had full race distance on it. The only thing that held us back was that I started getting cramps in my arms but I wasn't too worried. I was in the best shape of my life after spending the winter training with Anthony Peden, a top level international track cyclist, and the cramps cleared up at the next test at Phillip Island, which is where the bike really came good. We did

154 laps in three days there and both Loris and I were on lap record pace.

Obviously the bike had its strengths and weaknesses. We didn't have the grunt that everybody else had and it didn't want to come out of the corners, plus I think people realise now that it didn't handle all that well. What it did have was a lot of power from the mid range and I took full advantage of that when I could, as was the case down the front straight in Qatar in the opening race of the season. We'd had a good test there the week before so we knew we had good potential and we confirmed it in qualifying, when I was just 0.005 seconds off the pole position set by Valentino Rossi.

The race was pretty much a 22-lap battle between the two of us, Valentino passing me in the tight sections where I couldn't get the bike turned and me getting him back down the straight, simply because I couldn't get close enough to him coming out of the corners to do it anywhere else. Every time he came past me I had to wring the bike's neck just to stay close enough to him to get him back again on the straight. I knew that if I didn't do it every time then the gap would increase through the rest of the lap and I would lose touch. We gradually wore him down and on the last three laps he started to lose touch. I didn't realise I had a gap so I kept pushing and on the very last lap I set my fastest time of the race.

It was easy to the naked eye to differentiate the straight line speed advantage of the Ducati over the Yamaha but the average person can't see how badly a bike is handling in the corners, so naturally there were fans and people in the media saying, 'Stoner could only pass him on the straight.' I passed him there because it was the only place I could pass him, simple as that.

(If you look at videos of Dani and me you can see how we pick the bike up early and drive it out of the turn, which makes the bike look faster because you get more drive onto the straight. People constantly talk about Dani having a top-speed advantage because of his weight but it's not that, it's his riding style. It's what Dani has always done and it's one of the skills I had to work on throughout my career so that I could match him, or try to be even better if possible. Some riders, and I'm talking about good riders, try to get on the gas at the same point as Dani but they are still on the side of the tyre. They don't seem to grasp that you need to get the bike up on the fat part of the tyre to get the drive. Or maybe they grasp it but they just can't do it, I don't know.)

At the time, people refused to believe that Valentino could be beaten in a fair battle so all the credit went to the Ducati's top speed, rather than the hard work we had put into testing as a team or our performance around the rest of the circuit that was required to stay with Yamaha through the sections where it was far better suited. It was frustrating to us but I was happy. My competitive nature kicked in and I hoped I had made Honda and Yamaha sorry they'd not given me a chance. If I did that, then one of my goals for the season was already achieved. I genuinely wasn't expecting to win any more races.

I guess Valentino didn't think I would be a big threat either and he was quick to congratulate me after that one, all smiles and handshakes and a polite, 'Well done, Casey.'

We went to the next race at Jerez, where Loris had won the year before on the 990cc, but the 800cc just sucked there. It wouldn't stop bucking and weaving and the tyres didn't work either. I got caught up in a battle with a few guys in the early laps, lost some positions and even though the bike handled a little sweeter after the tyres wore down it was still hard to ride and our podium chance had gone.

Next up were races in Turkey and China, two circuits we'd only visited a couple of times previously and where I'd won in the 250cc class. Tracks that don't see much action don't have a lot of grip so it is hard to get confident and the European guys tend to struggle there. To me it didn't matter that there wasn't much grip and I didn't get too obsessed about the fact I didn't know the track. As always I just rode to what I could see and I was always extra competitive in those circumstances. I won by 6 seconds in Turkey and 3 seconds in China to open up a fifteen-point lead in the championship over Valentino. That started to make people notice us but still not in a huge way. As if the young Aussie could keep it up.

We picked up third in a really tricky wet race at Le Mans and then suffered our first bad result in Ducati's home Grand Prix at Mugello. We had a lot of rain during practice, didn't get our bike set up for the race and we were beaten by Alex Barros on the satellite Ducati. That weekend was a huge learning curve for me because it was the first time I had seen my team under real pressure. They spent all weekend working under the watchful eye of all the big bosses from Ducati and it changed the way they worked.

I like to think I can read people very well, especially people I get to study a lot, and when I come in during a session to make changes to the bike that is exactly what I am doing. The mechanics might think that because I have got my visor down I'm just sitting there doing nothing but I'm observing everything and I could see they weren't coping well with the pressure of having the big bosses watching over them.

I guess the fact we weren't happy with fourth place showed how far we had already come and at the next race in Barcelona we were fighting for the win again. I managed to take the lead from Dani after a few laps and after Valentino came through the pack by around mid-race distance it went down to another battle between me and him, with Dani just behind. All three of us at the front had our strong points and our weak points around the circuit so I was focused on trying to minimise my weak points and covering my lines. Again we had good speed down the long straight but we'd also set the bike up well for the braking points, so for Valentino to pass us he usually had to run wide on the exit and we were able to pass him back immediately. There were some nice passing manoeuvres going on everywhere, it was such a close race and no one could escape. Thankfully I managed to hold Valentino off on the last lap and won by 0.069 seconds.

That was a big win for us because we proved that we could win on European tracks and I was also proving that Valentino was not the unbeatable superhuman that people thought he was. Of course I had looked up to him as a rider for many years myself but to be honest there was no extra value in beating him as far as I was concerned. It didn't matter to me who finished second as long as I finished first and I never became obsessed with my rivals in a way that some riders do.

The problem with 'rivalries' is that if the other person is at the front then you're not happy unless you are up there with them. If your best hope in a particular race is to finish fourth then there is no point worrying about the guy with the 10-second lead, it's the people around you that you need to focus on beating. The flip side of that is that if your rival has a bad day at the office and is running in sixth place, does that mean you are going to be happy to finish fifth? For some riders that's what happens, but it is important to always be realistic about your own possibilities in every specific race.

I took my rivals on a day-to-day basis and in 2007 they varied more than people probably care to remember. One weekend it was Valentino but the next it could be Loris Capirossi, Dani Pedrosa, Chris Vermeulen, John Hopkins, Marco Melandri or Colin Edwards. It's an interesting statistic from that season that every one of the top twelve riders in the championship took at least one podium finish. If I had let myself become obsessed with Valentino, Loris or anybody else then maybe I would have allowed myself to be satisfied with results that were below my capabilities on that particular day. I just had to beat whoever was going to give me the toughest run.

At Donington Park you could have almost picked the podium finishers out of a hat. We'd had some problems with the electronics in qualifying and I was fifth on the grid for a race that would take place in soaking wet conditions, with Colin Edwards on pole. I got a perfect jump at the start, a perfect clutch release, but then I must have hit a white line and the rear spun up straight away but we still got into a reasonable position, twelfth I think, and we were able to pick our way through to second place behind Colin after five laps. Colin was riding nice and smooth but I knew I could go quicker and at half distance I passed him.

Then I saw the track getting drier and drier. I was worried about destroying the rear tyre, so I started going over all the wet patches to try and look after it, so that when we got to the last five laps it still felt pretty good and I was able to win by about 11 seconds. That was another massive victory for us because it proved to people that it wasn't just about horsepower. From Qatar to Barcelona people had been beating us with the same stick but at Donington Park you don't even get into top gear on a MotoGP bike.

That race was the twelfth in a row that had been won by a rider not starting from pole, which was a new record. People were making a big deal about it and questioning whether, psychologically speaking, it wasn't a good thing to qualify

on pole position at all. Maybe to the superstitious riders out
there it had become an issue but I have never allowed myself
to be affected by outside influences like that and I put an end
to the stat by winning from pole in the next round at Laguna
Seca in California.

It is amazing how many riders have superstitions, which to
me are completely ridiculous. Pretty much every one of them
has a little mascot or a lucky pair of undies that they once had a
good result in and have been stuck with ever since (so to speak!).
Superstition is basically just fear and as an athlete my view is that
by allowing it to enter your mind you are effectively handing
over control. My approach has always been to deliberately
tackle it by doing things differently to the last time, just to make
sure I don't get into a restrictive habit. Some riders look at their
qualifying position and think, I never go well from fifth position,
or arrive at a circuit thinking about past results there and say,
'I've never done well here before, it's not my favourite circuit.'
Effectively they have beaten themselves before they even start.

You have to be in the mindset that every day is a new
day, a new set of circumstances. Every corner is different,
every situation is different, and if you are not prepared to
open your mind to that then you will always struggle more
than necessary. You might have been through one particular
corner a thousand times before but with a slight change in
temperature, a new bike, a different tyre or a rider trying
to pass you on the inside it becomes a completely different
challenge and you have to be ready to deal with that.

That's why I could turn it on more than the other guys at a place like Laguna Seca, where the grip varied so much from year to year that it was almost like racing at a new track each time. To win there for the first time was really special and up to that point it was probably my best ever weekend in racing: I was fastest in every free practice and qualifying session, I won the race by almost 10 seconds and I extended my lead in the championship to forty-four points.

I also really enjoyed racing in front of the American fans, who had given me a lot of support at a time when I really needed it in 2006. Everywhere else I went I was getting criticised, I was a nobody, but at Laguna they respected every rider there for the racing and it made me feel very welcome. For some reason the American fans are a lot more impartial in their support of riders; they seem to love the sport first and the riders second, whereas for a large part of the European fans I would say it's the reverse. That kind of treatment has never changed and over the years we have made some great friends over there. Other than Australia it is the place I feel most at home.

Back in Europe the attention on me was growing. I'd hardly been bothered by people before but for some reason when you start winning people have this extra confidence to come up to you. It's like you have become public property through your own success. I would be sitting there having dinner with Adriana after a bad result (a bad result being third that season) and nobody would disturb us but if I won the race it was game on. It's weird. It seems that the less successful you are, the more right you have to your privacy. That's the way of the world I guess, but I wasn't going to stop winning just because I didn't like the attention.

After putting together another almost perfect race at Brno, our seventh win of the season, we went to Misano for Ducati's second home race. Even though it is technically the San Marino Grand Prix, Misano is in Italy and it is actually closer to Ducati's factory headquarters in Borgo Panigale than Mugello. It is also the circuit where they hold the huge World Ducati Week festival every summer, so this truly was their 'home' Grand Prix.

We knew why we'd stuffed up at Mugello and I was determined not to let the same thing happen again so I asked that no one other than team personnel be inside the garage during practice or qualifying. I said people were welcome to come in after for the debrief but otherwise I didn't want my mechanics under any more stress as it's already a tough job. We went to Misano without any real pressure on us because we had already exceeded our goals for the season but I knew there was a certain amount of expectation on me to win. It was a big weight off my shoulders when we did exactly that and with Dani crashing on the first lap and Valentino breaking down we could finally start thinking about the championship. With an 85-point lead and just five races to go it was suddenly a very real possibility that I could become MotoGP World Champion.

We picked up another podium in Portugal despite some problems with the clutch. After a few laps I worked out how to ride around it and I was catching Valentino and Dani at the end of the race but I ran out of time and there was too much at stake to take unnecessary risks. That result meant that we went to Japan leading by seventy-six points, essentially needing to finish ahead of Valentino to win the title at Motegi. The weekend didn't start well for us and Loris was adjusting to the track better than me. We just couldn't get the bike to stop pumping out of the corners and after qualifying in ninth place, easily my worst grid position of the season, any thoughts of the championship looked remote.

On race day we got lucky. It started raining and the race got under way in wet conditions, which gave me the chance to get up front quite early. I led for a lap before Melandri came past on lap five but I had a reasonably good feeling with the bike and I felt comfortable in second place. Things looked to be falling into our hands until the second half of the race, when the rain stopped, the track started to dry and the wet tyres started to wear out. At that point Valentino and Dani came past and I didn't really know whether to come in or not to change to my spare bike, which was fitted with slick tyres, until the team put 'box' on my pit board.

After we changed bikes there was something up with the steering damper and I couldn't tip into the corners like I wanted but luckily Valentino had a problem too and even though we crossed the line in sixth place we managed to finish ahead of him, which because of the problem with the steering was our only real target that day. Pretty much everybody had a disaster apart from the three who ended up on the podium: Capirossi, Toni Elías and Randy de Puniet.

It is hard to tell you how I felt at that moment in time. Despite having led the championship pretty much all season, the title crept up on us and I guess I didn't know what to think once we'd won it. I was happy, of course, but my overriding feeling after the race was annoyance about the result. I felt like I should have done more to win the championship, almost like I didn't deserve it because I'd finished sixth. You might think that is ridiculous but I wanted better results. Maybe it was just that I couldn't believe I was MotoGP World Champion, something I had been wanting and dreaming of since I was old enough to watch Mick Doohan on video and shaking a bottle of sparkling wine on my 50cc PeeWee.

That huge smile on my face on the podium told the story. Having Adri and Mum and Dad there made it even better. It was nice that Weap (Anthony Peden) was there too. For all of us it was a mixture of emotions: excitement, elation, relief and exhaustion after the adrenaline washed away.

Bronwyn Stoner: 'It was an extremely proud moment. I was just so happy for Casey. I think I had a delayed reaction because it wasn't until about half an hour later, when Livio Suppo walked up to me and gave me a hug to celebrate, that I burst into tears.'

There wasn't much time to let it all soak in because there were endless media appointments and then as soon as they were done we had to quickly pack everything up, get back to the hotel and grab our suitcases for the bus to Tokyo and a flight home to Australia. My outstanding memory of that trip is that the bus took us on all these back roads and I got crook because I still hadn't had anything in my stomach after the race. It was a really weird journey home but by the time we landed in Sydney everything started to sink in. It was pretty crazy to think that it was only seven years since I'd left the country through that very same airport with my mum, dad and a suitcase stuffed with a set of Terry Pav's old leathers having never raced a road bike.

I spent the week after we got back out at the Shamrock, cut off from everything, spending a bit of time with my parents and hanging out with Chaz, Adriana and my friend Chris Hillard from Alpinestars, who had been particularly supportive that season. After that we headed down to Newcastle for a few days of golf and sea fishing before catching a flight down to Melbourne to do some PR work for Dorna and the Australian Grand Prix Corporation. Day by day after winning the World Championship, it started to sink in more and more. We had a signing session in Federation Square and there was an incredible turnout of people queuing to meet me and congratulate me. I found it hard to understand why all these people were there just for me. It's not that I didn't appreciate it; it was just a weird thing that they cared and had taken time out of their busy day to come and see me. It was an awesome feeling and a very special moment.

That level of public attention came upon me very quickly. Compared to the European riders, who grow up under the spotlight and get used to the adulation from a young age, I had come from nowhere. The last time I had been in Australia I had been able to walk down the street without being recognised at all but now it seemed everybody knew who I was. It was kind of the same for Adri, who had become famous just for being my wife, which is a ridiculous concept, and we noticed it pretty much everywhere we went (though she does turn heads anyway!).

At first I wasn't sure how to deal with this new fame thing. My head was spinning with it all and I went along with a few ideas from fashion magazines like *Vanity Fair* wanting to do different photo shoots, dressing me up in outfits and things. Needless to say I absolutely hated all that. I don't like having my picture taken but these fashion shoots are insane and take so long. They'd be like, 'You must wear this, it's fashion!' But I don't give a rat's about fashion, as Adri or any of my friends will tell you! I still have a fleece sweater that George Lloyd gave me back in 2000 and it's probably my favourite item of clothing. Nowadays I won't do any of that stuff no matter how much somebody might be willing to pay. It isn't worth it. For me this sport was never about the money, it was about the passion.

It was amazing to go to Phillip Island with everything wrapped up and for the first time I was able to really enjoy riding the track with no pressure. With its long wheelbase the Ducati was well suited to the long, fast corners there and we already had a good setting from the pre-season test. We had a couple of issues in practice and I got held up in qualifying so we started from third place but I made one of my best ever starts, had the first corner to myself and was able to concentrate on getting the tyres warmed up and ready to go. Nicky pushed me hard for a while but it was just one of those days where everything was happening right for me and I had a ball. Winning at home was exceptionally sweet.

Being up on the podium in front of all those Australian fans was just unbelievable, I'd never felt anything like it. It was also cool because my teammate Loris, who had been good to me all season, was up there with me. With him having won the race in Japan, it was an incredible couple of weeks for the team and for Ducati.

Becoming MotoGP World Champion, winning my home Grand Prix and marrying the girl I loved weren't the only three dreams that came true in 2007. In the space of twelve months there had been quite a big turnaround in our financial situation and one more win that season, in Malaysia, helped contribute to a bonus package that amounted to four times my basic wage for the season.

I had to pinch myself at the end of that season: could it get any better! At that point, I could quite happily see myself spending the rest of my career with Ducati. Livio Suppo told us later that Filippo Preziosi, General Manager of Ducati

Corse, the arm of Ducati that deals with motorcycle racing, had put aside a 'crash budget' for me that season that was triple the usual budget for spare parts. That told me they were willing to deal with some crash damage in order to help me reach my potential. As it turned out I hardly crashed at all – just six times all season – but the important thing was that they showed commitment to my future when nobody else did. That meant a lot to me.

Livio says now: 'At that time, the Ducati Corse budget was not that big and we had to be prepared for, and try to prevent, any problems for Casey. It was great to spend the money we'd set aside (and more) to pay Casey's bonuses for wins and to see him win the title (and not have to use it for spare parts!). It was also important for us to show Casey we believed in him. With the right support from the company he wasn't crashing anymore, he was winning!'

With attitudes like that around me, I was looking forward to the next season to see what would unfold. I had no idea what was around the corner.

CHAPTER 10

A RUDE AWAKENING

One of the hardest things for anyone to do is to keep motivated after achieving their goals. That's perhaps magnified for sportspeople. You can spend your whole career chasing that one dream, visualising holding that one particular trophy, and then once you achieve it, what do you aim for next? I didn't think that was going to be a problem for me because I have always raced to win every race, from when I was first on the starting line at Hatcher's to the most recent event at Valencia, it's what matters most. When I line up on a starting grid there is nothing else on my mind, I'm not thinking of championship points, I'm concentrating on beating the riders on the track. But as much as I was still motivated, perhaps Ducati wasn't as hungry. I guess it's a natural reaction to become a little complacent after success and winning and maybe that is why they didn't seem as willing to put money into development. It is easy to take your eye off the ball while your competitors become more motivated to beat you. Looking back, we should have put more effort into improving the bike before the start of our World Championship defence in 2008.

A lot of things could have been done differently and increasing the budget to help Filippo and the team develop the bike was the main one. It didn't happen. We did a brief test with the Desmosedici GP8 at Jerez at the end of 2007 and I got a revised version in time for the start of testing at Sepang. They had changed a few small things on the rear end and in a lot of ways it was an improvement but it was very difficult to set up, which had been our biggest problem with the GP7. We had huge issues finding a base setting, issues that we were unable to fix in time for the start of the season, and the worst thing was that there was no second option. The bike we got for the test was the bike we would have for the rest of the season, other than the odd new part or engine mapping upgrade, which usually came too late anyway.

It was frustrating for me that Ducati had not devoted the time or resources over the winter to developing the bike and making sure it worked before they gave it to us. There were lots of things I asked to be changed, like altering the chassis stiffness a little, trying new triple clamps and providing some different swingarm options instead of just the one, but they didn't get the development done quickly enough and we soon fell behind our rivals. If we didn't get lucky and nail an idea first time then it took us too long to react and adapt.

Ducati is a small factory but that shouldn't be an excuse. They could have turned these things around if they wanted to. You can outsource and do all kinds of things to speed up development, but it all came down to a question of budget. I get that, but the success of 2007 should have been a platform to make things even better. Three years later Ducati proved they could do it, when they produced something like ten different chassis options in one year. Yes, I am comparing because I think I got four in the entire four years I was there and I am not sure why I didn't get the same commitment, especially after proving my worth as a rider and showing the investment could pay off.

As a newcomer to the team in 2007 I had bitten my tongue on a lot of matters and I was mostly happy with whatever I was given because I was a factory MotoGP rider for the first time. I was learning and taking it all in. But now I was World Champion and the goalposts had moved. They had to. One of the lessons I'd learnt was that I had to have a say and be listened to. It is why I was so happy working with Cristian the previous year because when I did have an opinion he wanted to hear it. Now I believed we needed significant backing to help us stay on top and challenge the factory Hondas and Yamahas but it didn't come. This time I didn't bite my tongue and I made my feelings known.

The lack of development with the bike wasn't the only thing that disappointed me at the start of that season. Marco Melandri had come in as my new teammate, which in itself wasn't a big problem because Marco is a nice enough guy, but he had come in on a big contract, signed back in 2006 when he was seen as one of the hottest young properties in MotoGP. It meant that even though I had won the championship in 2007, Marco still came in on a higher wage than me. That didn't feel fair. Money isn't everything but in MotoGP terms it is a measure of worth and it was unsettling that our victory didn't seem to be appreciated by everyone at Ducati as much as I thought it would.

There were other positive things happening early in 2008 that showed that people were taking notice of what we'd achieved. Probably the most surprising for me was my nomination as the NSW representative in the Young Australian of the Year Awards and even more surprising was the fact that I was officially announced the Young Australian of the Year and presented the award by then Prime Minister Kevin Rudd at an Australia Day celebration in Canberra. The Australian of the Year was country singer Lee Kernaghan, who as well as writing memorable songs had done a lot to raise money to help farmers hit by drought. We were both boys from the bush. There have been some very impressive people who have been Young Australian of the Year in the past, people like Lleyton Hewitt, Ian Thorpe and Cathy Freeman, to name just three, so I was in very good company and was a bit blown away by it all. It was a major event and there was a lot of media attention but I was honoured to be there to show that if you follow your dream, anything can happen. Who knows if a kid watching that day might have been inspired to chase their own dream? I hope so.

That year I was also awarded the Dawn Fraser Award, named in honour of Australian Olympic legend Dawn Fraser, at the Australian Sport Awards. It was pretty amazing to get that as well.

There wasn't much time to hang around in Australia once all the media events for Young Australian of the Year were done as we had to get ready for the opening round of the 2008 season in Losail, Qatar. We knew this was a track that could hide some of our problems and that proved to be the case. We were able to win an enjoyable race. I didn't get the best start and the tyres took a while to heat up so the first few laps were pretty hectic. It felt like a 125cc race with riders bumping fairings and I just tried to stay out of the way. On the eighth lap I saw my chance to get through, moving into the lead from fourth place, and from there I focused on setting my own pace.

Losail is a slippery circuit so we came off okay but we knew that as soon as we got to tracks with more grip we were in trouble because we still didn't have a base setting for the bike. That became very obvious in round two at Jerez. I ran off the track early in the race, which was my own fault, but I was running okay and still felt I could make it back to the top five when I went to overtake Shinya Nakano in the chicane and Chris Vermeulen came diving up the inside. We were three abreast and I ran off track again. I ended up eleventh, which was a major disappointment.

Things got worse at Estoril, where we struggled even more to find a setting and could only qualify ninth. The situation was no better for my teammate Melandri, who was down in seventeenth and having a nightmare of a time trying to adapt to the bike after moving from Honda. To make matters worse, one of Dorna's onboard camera's wiring box came loose during the race and was swinging around my handlebars. The cable was wrapping around the clutch lever and the box kept getting jammed in the steering column so I couldn't turn fully into the corners. I kept having to yank it out of the way but I was worried that if I pulled it out completely it might disconnect my electronics and shut the engine down. It destroyed our race and even though I received a written apology what we really needed were the points. I finished sixth.

Our troubles in the opening three rounds of 2008 coincided with the arrival of a new talent in the top class of MotoGP. Spanish rider Jorge Lorenzo had made a fantastic start to his rookie season, qualifying on pole in Qatar, where he finished second behind me, and taking his first win in Portugal. At that point he was leading the championship, level on points with Dani Pedrosa.

Despite my first impressions of Jorge in the 125ccs I got on pretty well with him during our days together in the 250cc class but after winning the World Championship in that category twice he seemed to me to have become arrogant beyond belief. I remember after Estoril he said something to Livio like, 'What happened to Stoner? A problem with the head?' He seemed to think he'd broken me in that race and that I was weak minded. He thought his success was the reason for my poor results and clearly had no idea about the problems we had with the camera, not to mention the bike.

A couple of weeks later we were in the pre-event press conference in Shanghai and Jorge made a smart remark like, 'Maybe the championship starts now for Stoner.' I couldn't believe it and I'd never known such arrogance before. But what Jorge didn't realise at the time was that his confidence, generated by his impressively fast adjustment to riding a MotoGP bike, was a big reason he was so quick in those early races. Confidence is an incredibly powerful tool in elite level sport but it can also be very dangerous, especially in motorcycle racing. He hadn't learnt that yet, but he would.

When a rider starts to build confidence they push the limits of the bike further and further until they find speed they thought they never had, speed that other riders find it impossible to live with. It is a fine line though. The problem is that as the level of confidence continues to increase so does the level of risk and before a rider knows it he is past the limit. Sooner or later reality bites and in motorcycle racing it bites hard. This is why I am always careful to be a realist. If I know I have the tools to get the job done then I can be confident, but I am careful never to ride on confidence alone.

Unfortunately for Jorge, just 48 hours after he made those remarks in China it became clear he was in over his head, literally, and he suffered one of the biggest crashes I have ever seen. In the split second that he hit the ground and fractured both of his ankles he also shattered the one thing that had taken him to the top of the championship. Once his confidence was gone he had nothing left to fall back on and he couldn't have copped any more of a beating than he did that season. He had crash after crash, bringing him back to earth so hard that he seemed to become scared of the bike. For a while his results were pretty ordinary, considering the equipment he was on.

If there was one good thing to come out of that whole season it was that Jorge seemed to realise what he'd been like and the next time I had much to do with him he was completely different. Since then he has become one of the guys that I respect the most out of anybody in the entire paddock. We had similar issues as teenagers, and though we are very different we can relate to each other in lots of ways. I've realised we just deal with things differently; for example Jorge's defence mechanism is to be cocky, whereas I become more introverted and shut down, but we both can be misinterpreted because of how we appear.

The thing I admire most about Jorge is that he admitted

Adri and I have been blessed with the opportunity to see many parts of the world, like Rome (*above*), but the place I always love coming home to is my farm in northern New South Wales (*below*).

After finishing second to Jorge Lorenzo in Portugal I held off Valentino Rossi (46) and Dani Pedrosa (3) for the win next time out at Phillip Island. It was a sweet moment for me. I'd gone from severe ill health from undiagnosed lactose intolerance in 2009 and thinking my career was over to being back on top of the podium at my home Grand Prix.

© Andrew Northcott

Finally riding in the same Repsol Honda Team colours as Mick Doohan in 2011 was a dream come true. My challenge was to rekindle the success they'd enjoyed with him and we started out perfectly with a win in Qatar. We took our sixth win of the season in round eleven at Brno to open up a good advantage at the top of the championship.

© Andrew Northcott

On my 26th birthday I won my fifth straight home Grand Prix at Phillip Island and also my second World Championship. I also won the Constructors' Championship for Honda. Perfect days like this don't come around too often! It had been a long and difficult journey for my parents and my wife but they always believed I would become World Champion.

© Andrew Northcott

Me with my friends Chris Hillard (*left*) from Alpinestars and Rhys Edwards (*right*).

Mick Doohan did a couple of demo laps on my bike before my final race at Phillip Island. As my all-time hero and a five-time World Champion I couldn't have left it in better hands!

The team I'd worked with became like family. Piero (holding Ally) was like another grandpa to Ally. At dinnertime he would offer to look after her while Adri and I ate.

Having a corner named after me at Phillip Island was an incredibly proud moment for the whole Stoner family. The commemorative plaque has 27 diamonds in it – as you can see, Ally already has expensive taste!

© Andrew Northcott

I learnt to ski in 2008 at Madonna di Campiglio during the team launch. Now that I've stepped away from MotoGP I am looking forward to improving my skiing and snowboarding skills to the point where I can heli-ski anywhere in the world.

Have I mentioned I love fishing? My mate, Australian Fishing Champion Jason Wilhelm (*top*) is partly responsible. He's introduced me to many of his fishing friends. Spending time with professionals like him, Paul Worsteling (*middle*) and Carl Jocumsen (*below*) has been great and I am keen to learn as much as I can about different types of fishing. These photos are deceptive – I know already that you don't always catch fish. It helps if you are with people who know all the tricks!

Spending time with my little girl, Ally, is what is important to me now. I'm trying to teach her to be interested in the outdoors — we are at Bass Pro, a great outdoor store in the US. Can never start too young!

After I retired we had a family holiday in the Cook Islands. My idea of paradise: Ally, Adri and somewhere to fish!

his character flaws and made an effort to change, which is impressive for a guy in his position and not something many people are prepared to do. He lives in his own world a lot of the time and he still has that little bit of arrogance about him but he is a massive talent and once you get to know him he's a very good guy, a great character and nothing but a positive for the sport of motorcycle racing.

My on-track battles with Jorge would intensify in later years but in 2008 we had our own problems to fix. We rode around set-up issues to pick up third place in China before a disastrous race at Le Mans. During the race my bike completely cut out and I had to roll it back into pit lane, pushing it the rest of the way to be able to swap to my second bike. The rules state that if you swap bikes the second bike must have different tyres to the first. I had come in on slicks so I had no choice but to exit on wets. There were a couple of drops of rain but it was our only option so we had to hope for the best. We struggled home in sixteenth place. It was the first time I'd failed to score points with Ducati.

A two-day test at Le Mans helped us detect a faulty component in the engine and at Mugello we made some real progress with the setting, finishing second there and then qualifying on pole position in Barcelona, where we really hit our stride. We finished third in that race and made our biggest breakthrough yet with the electronics in the post-race test. Finally we had a bike that wasn't trying to throw us off and wasn't pumping in every corner. There was a lot smoother power delivery. We were able to take three wins in a row at Donington, Assen and Sachsenring, closing the gap between me and Valentino – who was at the top of the championship – to twenty points.

While I wasn't focused on any rivalry that was starting to develop between me and Valentino Rossi, the same could not be said for the fans. Around that time I became the target of a lot of hatred, especially from Valentino's many followers. The first signs of it began to show in 2007 when I started beating him. Mum used to get some nasty emails.

Sadly, she remembers it well. 'All Casey's fan mail used to come to our computer and I used to read all these horrible emails. There weren't many of them but the ones we did receive were awful. I had to learn to ignore them; hit delete and forget it. Eventually you develop a thick skin because you have to, for self-preservation.'

I hated that my mother was reading stuff like this but it didn't bother me personally most of the time. There was one incident at Donington Park that has stuck in my mind though. After I won the race I was waving to the crowd on the cool-down lap and I caught sight of a lady, who must have been in her sixties, giving me the 'V' sign – and it wasn't for victory! I couldn't believe it. I was shocked because she looked like someone's grandma. I'm not saying this about all British fans, not at all, but there is certainly a number of them who treat racing like some kind of war and have to have an enemy in their sights. For so many years Valentino had been their hero and anybody who came along to challenge him was the bad guy, whether it was Max Biaggi, Sete Gibernau, Jorge Lorenzo or myself.

There was an even worse incident a year later, again at Donington, when I was really sick. I had no strength and lost the front in either Coppice or McLeans corner, I can't remember which, and crashed during practice. Riding back along the service road on the back of the scooter that picked me up there were people swearing and spitting at me, a couple of them even jumped in front of us trying to make the guy riding the scooter lose control and crash.

A day or two earlier in the 'Day of Champions' auction, when all the riders go along and donate signed memorabilia in order to raise money for the Riders for Health charity, I had been booed as I stepped onto the stage. That didn't feel great, I have to tell you. After that I refused any physical appearances at that event. I continued to donate items for the charity but there was no way I was going back on that stage; not because I couldn't handle being booed but because I wasn't going to give those brainless people what they wanted and cop more abuse. It probably didn't help my popularity in the UK and I was sorry I couldn't acknowledge the true British fans who wanted to see me up there, and who sent emails apologising for the behaviour of this minority of people. They told me they were ashamed of their compatriots.

I respect that people are enthusiastic in their support of a rider but for it to spill over into open animosity for the guys racing against him is wrong. For me to get that kind of reaction in a country where I had spent so much time and had a lot of friends, a country where my dad's family came from, was particularly hurtful. Maybe someone who could put on the charm when they need it regardless of sincerity could have turned the situation around but I don't have that skill. I am who I am and I can't fake feeling good or liking something I don't.

The way fans treated me seemed to get worse after the famous battle between me and Valentino in the next round at Laguna Seca, a race that will probably always be remembered for Rossi's pass on me in the Corkscrew. Obviously I wasn't happy about that particular move but there were other things that happened that weren't caught on camera.

The truth is that for a lot of the race Valentino was riding really well. He did a fantastic job. Our bike wasn't very nimble and we only had one line to ride around that circuit and he was smart and realised that. Nowadays he knows it only too well but with the Ducati you don't have many options when it comes to getting it around the corner. Valentino knew that by getting in front of me at every opportunity he could make it very hard for me to get back in front of him. Whenever I did take the lead his only option was to hit back immediately to stop me from getting away. A lot of it was fair racing, he was out-braking me on the inside and riding better than me around a lot of the track. If it had all been like that I would cop it sweet. But a couple of moves off camera added to my frustration. I risked running off the track, and racing at the limits like that as we were I even became worried about my safety.

I first became aware of Valentino pushing like this back in 2006, when he put a couple of passes on me in races and in practice that I thought were a bit too much. I had nothing but respect for him before that but those choices made me wary. It is hard to see it on television, in the same way that it's hard to appreciate how fast we are going. But to ride as close as we do at that speed you have to really respect and trust each other. We get to understand the body language of other riders and learn there are ways to pass someone without making contact, without pushing people onto the kerb, but somehow Valentino and I weren't on the same wavelength and as a result I always felt I had to be super-alert when I raced him.

We had a lot of great battles over the years but there were occasions where he would try different tactics that surprised me. Laguna Seca was one of the occasions where he had to get a result. After winning three races in a row I was on a roll and we had carried our form to America. I was fastest by more than half a second in every free practice session and comfortably set pole ahead of Valentino, with a race pace that was a good second quicker than his. Riding what I considered overly aggressive was the only way that he could win that day unless I crashed, so that's what he did.

It is funny how many people use that one race as an argument to prove that Valentino had the better of me, regardless of the number of times I beat him before and after. But I know that whole experience made me a lot stronger as a rider and as a person. I gained a better understanding of how to deal with other riders when they push like that. From that point on maybe I didn't always ride as gentlemanly as I had done in the past and I decided that if I saw a space I was going to take it. To the riders who showed respect I was the same as always but for those who didn't show respect, I was over being nice to them. That change in mindset definitely helped me in certain situations over the following seasons.

In the next round at Brno the bike was working pretty well all weekend and I qualified on pole by over a second in the wet but made a mistake on the seventh lap of the race, lost the front and slipped off. Looking at the lap times I could have probably still finished on the podium if I got back on the bike but it wouldn't restart. The reason why pretty much summed up my season. After examining the bike back in the garage the team showed me a rock, the exact size and half-moon shape to fit into the butterfly valves and jam them closed. There was probably no other rock in that gravel trap that would have done it. It was just not meant to happen.

Lots of people thought I crashed that day because Valentino had got into my head but that is not the case and they were reading far too much into it. When I go out to race I try to win, it's as simple as that. I'm not looking at the bigger picture, at the championship or things that have gone on before with other riders. Maybe those side stories make the racing more interesting for the spectator but from my perspective I just enjoy winning so much that it surpasses any other feeling or intention on the day. I don't care what happened last week, what happened yesterday or what happened that morning. I want to win and that's it, which is why I have been able to come back from big crashes during practice, qualifying or warm-up and still perform on a Sunday afternoon. Some riders, if they have a big one in practice then that's it, you can write them off for the race. But not me. People said at the time I was mentally weak but I don't know what they based that on. I always felt like I was one of the mentally toughest out there. No matter what beat me down, or what was going on away from the track in my private life, I could switch everything off for the race and concentrate purely on that.

But there was something weird happening at Brno, which was nothing to do with the bike or my head; I'd started to feel a bit of discomfort in the wrist I had damaged back in 2003. Then at Misano the whole thing collapsed, to the point that I could actually pull my thumb back to make a 180-degree angle with my forefinger. We had some scans, which showed that the staple that was supposed to have been holding my scaphoid together had not set properly. As a result the bone had broken up into four pieces and I needed a bone graft to fix it back together. Livio wanted me to get the operation done straight away but I refused. There was no way I wanted to rush into surgery again and besides, an operation now would rule me out for at least a couple of races and definitely spell the end to my championship. We decided to keep going and wait until the end of the season. Maybe it wasn't the right decision but I was there to race and I was sure I could, even with a buggered wrist.

I had to have my wrist strapped up so tightly for the race at Misano, just to keep my thumb in position, that I couldn't use my fingers or hand properly. It gave me bad arm pump (basically your arms pump up full of blood and the muscles swell and block the nerves, leading to a loss of power and control) but it was the only way to keep the wrist from collapsing under braking. Also, in certain positions on the bike the nerves would get trapped by the floating bone and send a shooting pain up my arm. It held up pretty well in the race but unfortunately we'd made a bad decision with the front tyre, putting a lap on it in the morning warm-up to scrub it in. It was a tactic we had tried before with no problem but this time it didn't feel right from the start and it let go after six laps.

Still, we came back to win two more races before the end of the season, including my home Grand Prix at Phillip Island, and I finished the 2008 season as runner-up to Rossi on 280 points, a new record for a rider not winning the championship.

At the end of the season Adri and I went back to Italy so I could have the bone graft at a specialist hospital in Modena. Here, the staple was removed, along with a couple of pieces of floating bone, and replaced by tiny screws. After that we headed back to Switzerland, where Adri and I had set up home, for some rest and recuperation. The operation meant I wasn't able to train properly for the majority of the off-season but I was still focused on my fitness so was doing what I could to maintain that. At the start of the 2009 season I was the fittest I'd ever been.

The GP9 was probably the best bike I had at Ducati. It featured a carbon chassis that we'd first tried at the Barcelona test in 2008 and we'd begged to have it for the second half of the season. It would have given us a much better chance of challenging for the championship but there was no way we were getting it that season. At Ducati we would get a lot of things that we asked for but unfortunately always several months too late, by which time you needed the next thing and would have to wait another six to eight months.

We had some teething problems with the new bike at the start of the 2009 season and it still wasn't the easiest thing to set up by any means but we managed to get it moving okay. After winning the opening race in Qatar we had an issue with the brakes in Japan and salvaged fourth. We got a podium at Jerez where the bike never, ever worked, and then had a problem with the steering damper at Le Mans and finished fifth. On paper it wasn't our best start to a season but our rivals had their problems too and a first win for us at Mugello in round five put us four points clear of Lorenzo at the top of the standings. We knew that this bike had real potential and we still hadn't got to the tracks where we usually excel at, so we were feeling confident that we stood a very strong chance of winning the championship back.

Then something started to go wrong that I couldn't explain. After the race at Mugello I was a lot more tired than I had ever felt in a race. I was surprised because I had been training well with Anthony, so I didn't really understand it and just shrugged it off as a one-off. Then during warm-up on the morning of the next race in Barcelona I was worn out after just a few laps. I was so tired I went back to bed and slept for two hours.

That afternoon was when it really hit, exactly as everybody saw on the television. It didn't come on slowly, the fatigue hit me with a big bang after about five laps. One minute I was okay and then suddenly I had so little strength that I was just hanging on to the bike by the end of the race, so exhausted that I could barely get off it in parc fermé. I couldn't walk or talk, I just wanted to throw up and almost collapsed on the podium.

I had seen doctors about some tiredness back in Australia in 2006. They said I had chronic fatigue syndrome, which they put down to a combination of my diet and my busy schedule. But this time it was far more serious and it seemed that no matter what I tried to do to make myself better I only got worse. I started having more recovery drinks made up of milk and whey powder and my condition continued to deteriorate even more rapidly. I didn't suspect that what I was doing to help was causing even more problems.

We battled on and I managed to pick up third at Assen, fourth at Laguna Seca and fourth at Sachsenring but by

the end of every race I was struggling just to stay upright.
I couldn't concentrate for more than a few laps at a time
and I had become something I hate even more than losing:
I'd become a danger to other riders. Nobody knew more
than me that things weren't good but the tension started to
build with Ducati as well. I'd seen every doctor and specialist
they had wanted me to see, in Europe and in the USA and I
had every test imaginable. I felt like a pin cushion but they all
came back saying it was in my head or that I had a hormone
imbalance, which was nonsense. There were lots of theories
but no diagnosis and nothing I tried made me feel better.
Ducati weren't happy and I could feel that but when they
started making announcements about my condition without
my consent, that really disappointed me.

Things reached a head at Donington Park, where there
was some confusion on the grid over tyre choice because it
had started raining. The sensible option was to go with slicks,
which is what all the other guys at the front were running,
and then come in to change if the rain got heavier. On the
other hand if the rain came quickly then it would be a massive
advantage to be on wets from the start. It was a big gamble
but I insisted on running wets.

To my team and to the outside world it looked like a crazy
decision but as far as I was concerned I was playing my last
card. I knew that if it stayed dry I had no chance anyway
because the physical demands of riding the bike on slicks
are so much higher, I didn't think I could make it to the end.

My only hope of staying in the championship was to pray for a downpour, pick up some points and try to figure out my problem before the next race.

Because the team were convinced that everything was in my head they clearly weren't happy with my choice and they let me know about it. We had won a title together, I had been equal top in the championship after Barcelona and I'd given everything I had for us to do that. Now I needed Ducati to stand by me but I felt like they were giving up on me instead. They started talking to me about my training, telling me what I needed to do to get my fitness levels back up, but none of them had any idea what I was going through. I could have skipped training for two years and still feel stronger than I did at that point. It was all ridiculous. It was very frustrating because there was something physically wrong with me but no one knew what it was, it would have been disturbing if I was happy while all this was going on.

Colin Stoner: 'I could see the desperation in Casey at Donington and the previous rounds. He was very ill and, after consulting Dr Halpin in Australia, Bronwyn and I talked with Casey and Adri and it was decided the best thing was to bring Casey home for further medical tests and rest. He would miss Brno, Indianapolis and Misano but hopefully it would mean he could find out what was wrong and get treatment.'

The news of me heading back to Australia didn't go down well and I got an email from Claudio Domenicali, who was

CEO of Ducati Corse, basically saying, 'I hope you don't expect to get paid for this.' Filippo Preziosi and Livio Suppo stayed loyal to us the whole time and so did Carlo Bonomi, who was president of the investment company that owned Ducati, but unfortunately the same was not true for most of their upper management. It was extremely disappointing not to have the support of my employers during one of the most difficult times of my life. But I knew that if I didn't get to the root of my problem then I was facing the end of my career, it was as simple as that.

I went back to Newcastle to see Dr Neil Halpin, a specialist sports physician, who had been my doctor since 2006. Neil is a fantastic doctor but also a great guy and somebody who always makes me feel very much at ease. He is also the official doctor for the Sydney Roosters and Newcastle Knights rugby league teams so he is used to dealing with professional athletes and I trusted his opinion more than anybody else's.

Dr Halpin states now: 'There had been accusations or the suggestion that it was a psychological matter, that Casey'd lost interest in his profession, but I saw no evidence of that whatsoever. There was a suggestion also of depression but I always think that in sport, particularly, depression is a chicken-and-egg problem. If you can't do your job because you are ill and the people who are supposed to trust you lose their faith in you, it would be no surprise that you might become depressed. But I don't know if that was the case. Melancholy depression is a biochemical disorder but Casey didn't strike me as being primarily depressed. My own impression was that he had a physical condition and any hint of depression and the ramifications of it were secondary to that. He was very weak, he didn't look well at all. We tested him for every infection, every endocrinological disorder. I sent him to a consultant physician who tested him for things I've never even heard of, and I've been a doctor for thirty-five years. We drew a blank with just about everything.'

I spent a week having tests and scans. Two of the tests I had to do, for lactose and gluten intolerance, were two- or three-week processes that required experimenting with being on and off them. I had to go on a strict elimination diet to try and pinpoint any problems that could be food related. During that time I was getting hounded by the press so in the end Dad said, 'Look Case, just get away.' Adri thought it was just what I needed, so I took off with my cousin Mark and did a trip I had always wanted to do, camping and fishing around the Northern Territory. We didn't have much time to prepare but we packed up, jumped in the four-wheel drive with the camper trailer and bolted, away from everybody and everything.

I flew back down to Sydney for some more tests and then flew back up to Darwin to meet Mark and continue our trip. I had no idea that my decision to get away was going to be so controversial. While I was up in the Northern Territory somebody took a photo of me fishing, which then appeared in the media, and I came back to another hounding. People took that photo as proof I wasn't sick, that it was all in my head, that I should retire. I wasn't aware of it at the time but back in Europe I was getting even more stick, some of it from people who are supposed to know what they are talking about. I got ripped into by the press, by my peers and by former riders.

Kevin Schwantz, one of my favourite riders and someone I'd looked up to, used superbikeplanet.com to put the boot in: 'What I've heard and what I've seen is that Casey's been struggling with some type of an illness, whether it was a stomach bug or whatever ... the last one I went to at the Czech Republic he wasn't there, still with no form of illness that's been diagnosed by any doctors that I've heard, anyway. As a rider, my gut feeling is Casey needs to be out there competing. This championship, when he made a tyre choice at Donington which seemed to be a little bit off of the norm, had him right at the top of it. I mean, he didn't need to be making a gamble on tyres like that when he was in the championship hunt. For me that told me there was more going on with Casey than just "you know I don't really feel all that good but I'm finding a way to perform." And for me, to have signed a contract whenever it was, beginning of this year, beginning of last year, whenever it was, you're signing a contract to compete unless something is medically wrong with you. I'm out there doing the best that I can, whether I can give 100% every weekend is kind of another question. For me it's a real disappointment.'

Those comments really upset me and I lost a lot of respect for Kevin because of them. For him to say something like that was another example showing me that experience counts for nothing. The media often turn to former riders for an opinion, which would be a good thing if they stuck to what they know. Sadly, often their opinions are outdated and they don't know the half of it but talk endlessly as if they do. In this case, Kevin Schwantz knew nothing about my medical condition and shouldn't have commented on something he knew nothing about. For somebody who has been through a lot of tough times himself with injuries and such, you would think he might understand. It was disappointing but he wasn't the only one who had something to say.

Everybody had their own opinions. A rider doesn't go from being ultra-competitive for two years and then just drop off the face of the earth because it's 'in his head'. It is absurd for anybody to even think that. If it was depression, lack of motivation or fear I would have said. People like Chaz and Leon believed in me because they'd known me for so many years and knew I wouldn't just switch off like that. But not many people stood by me through the uncertainty. Adri, Mum and Dad, Filippo, Livio, Chris Hillard, I could practically count them all on two hands. Even within my Ducati racing team, which only a year before had felt like family, there were doubters. I think a few of the guys believed me when I said something was physically wrong but others didn't. Some of the friendships I had grew stronger through all this, and some of the friendships disappeared. In a way that was a good thing. It gave me a better perspective of what racing meant to me and what people really thought of me, who I could trust.

There were certainly people I couldn't trust at Ducati. While I was away they offered Jorge Lorenzo a contract for double the money I was on to come in and replace me. They'd told me when we signed a contract for 2009 and 2010 that they didn't have any more money for me, didn't have money for development but now suddenly they could afford to shell out like that for another rider? Considering what we had achieved together, I couldn't believe it. I felt I had been stabbed in the back by the people I trusted and who were supposed to trust me. I was blown away, and not in a good way.

At the time I had no idea all this was unfolding. After two weeks up in Darwin I went back on lactose and that night I was as sick as a dog. I couldn't get out of bed, I lost my voice and was stuck in bed for days not feeling well enough to do much. The doctor had told me to look out for a reaction but I was expecting something far less severe so I genuinely didn't put two and two together straight away. The doc had thought there was more chance of it being gluten if it was food related so we were focusing more on that. A week later I tried going back on gluten but there was no direct reaction so we ruled that out. I was still tired from what we thought was the flu that I'd caught and I couldn't even walk up a slight slope without puffing like somebody who's been smoking their whole life.

By the time we headed back to Europe I was still feeling lethargic and I had started to lose faith that I was ever going to get to the bottom of it and feel well again. We arrived a week before the race in Portugal and I said to Adriana, 'You know, because I got so sick after Darwin I never actually finished off the lactose test properly.' We decided to try it again, just to be sure. As the week went on and lactose started to leave my system I started to feel better. Because I hadn't done anything to exert myself that week I wasn't sure if it was working or not. It wasn't until the Friday, when I got back on the bike that I realised there was a massive difference.

I struggled a bit with arm pump in the first free practice, which was to be expected because I hadn't been on the bike for two months, but otherwise I felt good and there was no hint of the extreme exhaustion from the last time I had ridden at Donington Park. I finished fourth quickest, 0.7 seconds off the fastest time, and on the second day I got faster, finishing second in free practice and third in qualifying. On the Sunday morning I was fastest in the warm-up, two-tenths of a second quicker than Dani, but still I couldn't be sure of my exact condition until we had gone the full race distance.

There was no beating Jorge that day and he took off at the front but after battling with Dani for the first few laps I got myself up to second place and created a 1.5-second gap. I kept hammering the lap times, which were only around a tenth of a second slower than Jorge, and all the while I was expecting to die halfway through the race but it never came. I kept hammering the whole race, stayed comfortably in front of Dani and brought it home in second place. That was a fantastic feeling, indescribable really. From thinking that my career could be over for good I now had reason to believe that I could come back stronger and better than ever. I had something to prove, too.

Before going back to Australia for the next race at Phillip Island we decided to try lactose again, just to confirm that it definitely was the source of the problem. Within the next day or two I started losing my usual energy. In a way, this made us happy because I could finally confirm what the problem was. After that it was like a whole new world. For ten years it had seemed to me that a lot of food tasted the same and I could go a whole day without eating and not be hungry. Once I knew what the problem was and knew what to do everything started to smell and taste good. Even the amount I ate doubled!

Adriana could see a huge difference almost straight away. And not just physically: 'I love cooking but any time I'd ever put anything on the table for Casey in the past, even though he was always polite, I could tell he wasn't enthusiastic about it. I was like, "I just cooked that for you!" Now he actually started to enjoy my cooking and that was one of the happiest days of my life.'

For a while I didn't go near lactose at all but then we discovered Lacteeze tablets and with them I can pretty much eat anything I want. Adri makes tacos, creamy pasta sauce with vegies and traditional Slovakian dishes like *svieckova*, which is beef in a carrot sauce, and knedle bread. I could finally eat my favourite dessert – sticky date pudding with custard – without getting sick afterwards. I was always pretty skinny and even though I trained my backside off I never put any weight on. But now my body suddenly started filling out and I started to actually put weight on and gain some body fat, which I'd never had before.

I know now that there are so many people out there with lactose intolerance who don't even know it. Other people I am sure think they are lazy but it might just be their diet. As humans we are not made to have lactose and supposedly 90 per cent of the world's population is intolerant to different degrees. Some people get crook stomachs, which is what I had for years and years until it started affecting me in an even more extreme way, but different people have different tolerance levels.

Looking back I don't know how I managed to train as hard as I did and compete without the right energy. Anthony and I were always surprised that I could just run lean. My body was so economical, it was like a car running on no fuel. But now I go training and I eat to train. I can come back in from a 90-km bicycle ride and eat a huge bowl of pasta and then eat a full lunch a couple of hours later. It's amazing the difference in my body once we uncovered and dealt with the problem.

Before Estoril I hadn't trained in eight or nine months but I came back stronger than ever. It was partly down to my base fitness but mainly it was a mental thing that goes back to my approach of not allowing outside factors to influence my state of mind. Some riders get so obsessed with physical fitness it becomes like a superstition. If they can't train they think that they're not going to be fit enough to fight in the race. But if you're relaxed and happy with the work you have done over the years then there is no need to panic.

I learnt about this from two people at opposite ends of the scale: Aaron Slight, who was a fitness fanatic, and Colin Edwards, who barely trains at all. Both riders were extremely fast but I don't think either approach did them any favours in the long run. There has to be a happy medium. Anthony always says, 'Happy mind, fast body.' You have to train, there is no way around it, but you can't become obsessed with it. If you allow that to happen then you forget what's important. Nowadays riders are getting overly obsessed with cycling. They focus so much on being a cyclist that they forget about their upper body. Having strong legs and cardiovascular fitness is important but there is so much more to riding a bike than that. Generally my training combines cycling with circuit training, supersets, things like that. If you train hard enough during the winter you can just top it up during the season.

Anthony Peden: 'Casey is an amazingly focused and driven individual, without question one of the hardest-working athletes I have had the pleasure to work with; however, his strengths don't stop there. His ability to focus and turn adversity into results while pushing well past limits still amazes me. It takes more to be a champion than to just be fast and

Casey has proven what a champion he is time and time again.'

As a racer, mental strength is just as, if not more important than physical strength. During my absence in 2009 my place on the factory bike was taken by Mika Kallio, my former 125cc teammate at KTM. Mika had come into MotoGP that year on a satellite Ducati with the Pramac team and had some reasonable results, so I guess he thought that jumping on my bike was going to be a huge step up. Unfortunately for him he found out it was exactly the same, so he went from thinking he was doing a decent job on an average bike to realising that I was winning races on the same package. I don't know Mika well personally so I can't say for sure but to me that experience seemed to set in motion quite a dramatic decline over the next couple of years and his career went backwards.

Livio once said to me that when a rider is not having success they have to find an excuse because the alternative is to accept they are not good enough. If they do that then it is hard to find the motivation to keep digging. Why even bother to keep on racing if you know you can't win? He says riders always have to have that in them. I find a lot of truth in that, but personally I also think it is a weakness. If a rider truly believes that the bike is the problem and not them, this gives them confidence to keep going. But I have never needed that confidence because my approach is to adapt myself if necessary. I have no problem admitting if it is me who needs to be faster. If the bike had problems I tried to ride around them, not point them out and use them as an excuse.

Livio Suppo: 'Casey is different from any other rider. He is so honest, with himself and others, that for him it is impossible to make excuses. This is one of his personality traits I admire the most.'

This honesty can sometimes get me in trouble but it is one of the main reasons why I was able to ride the Ducati competitively when nobody else could. Whatever was wrong with that bike, I didn't let it defeat me. If anything it actually motivated me even more to keep trying. If I made a mistake when the bike was good and ruined a weekend I didn't look at anybody but myself to blame. I got a lot of criticism over the years for being honest because I always felt I could do better. Even if I won the race, if I had made mistakes it was important for me to admit them and address them for next time instead of congratulating myself for being the best on that particular day.

There were times when I would be 2 seconds a lap quicker than any other Ducati on track but I never used that as a reason to stop trying. I could have easily done that and everybody would have forgiven me, but if anything it would make me think that 2 seconds wasn't enough – I'd want to be 3 seconds faster. That desire to constantly challenge myself when there was no other challenge around, goes right back to those first days I ever rode a dirt-bike with just myself or my sister for company, this was the foundation of every success I ever had.

After that podium in Portugal we picked up back-to-back wins at Phillip Island and Sepang, meaning that I still had a mathematical chance of challenging Jorge for second in the championship going into the final round at Valencia, which is amazing considering how much racing we had missed that season. Unfortunately that chance disappeared before the race even started because of a faulty tyre warmer. Unbeknown to me or the team I had been sitting on the grid for twenty minutes with a cold tyre and I crashed on the warm-up lap. It wasn't the ideal way to finish the season but it didn't really matter in the grand scheme of things. I was back to competing and knew I could do better.

The most important thing was that we had salvaged my career and I could now look forward to trying to win the championship in 2010. One thing I was clear about, though, was that I wanted to win it for myself and for my team, but not for the company. After the way they'd behaved I had pretty much decided that I was through with Ducati and even though they put a new contract in front of me, for 2011 and 2012, it was going to take a much grander gesture to make me stay.

I told them I wanted them to show me what I meant to them. 'What do you mean?' they said. 'That's up to you,' I told them. I gave them months to do it and nothing happened. In the end I had to spell it out. I said, 'Rip up my current contract and show me what I am worth to you.' They wouldn't do it, and that told me all I needed to know. Up until then there was a chance that I'd stay but that effectively made my decision easy. I decided to follow the one dream I had left in racing and go where I had always wanted to go. I signed a contract for the 2011 season with Honda in the second round of the 2010 season at Jerez.

I should have expected it but once that deal was done Ducati shut down development on our side of the garage. It sucked because once again we had started the year with a bike that wasn't great. We had been forced to run a new 48mm Öhlins front fork that everybody else was using, which was better over the bumps but because we already had a carbon fibre chassis it added to the stiffness. We ended up having a lot of front-end crashes, always in the middle of the corner. I could load it up fine on the way in but when you were in the middle of the corner, controlling the throttle, that's when it would go and there was no way to feel it or get it back. We tried so many different things to sort it out but particularly at the beginning of the season we just couldn't get to grips with it.

I went down in Qatar and didn't have a clue what happened, same thing at Le Mans, and after five rounds we were still looking for our first podium. We'd gone back to 42mm forks in the fourth round at Mugello, which were a lot better but because we had such a stiff chassis it didn't want to work with a soft fork either. We learnt a lot about setting the bike up and eventually got it working with a very unique setting, which allowed us to get on the podium at Assen and for the next four races after that.

The year dragged out and I didn't think I was going to get a win but I was never going to give up. My approach of pushing the bike to the front even if it wasn't really capable had not changed from when I was a kid and I had my fair share of crashes as the year went on. People could criticise that all they wanted but it was a method that had taught me to ride around problems and push a bike. The thing was that I knew how to push a bike close to the limit, whereas some riders would not be willing to get to that point.

Our first win of the season finally came in the thirteenth round at Aragon in Spain, where we made big changes to the offset of the bike. We moved the front end further forward and moved the rear forward too, which gave us more grip on the rear and created more flex in the chassis. We made the whole bike longer, as long as we could possibly go and with as much rake as we could manage, just to get some flex into the front end. It was a little bit strange to ride at first – the front wanted to come around and hit the apex a bit late – but finally we had some feeling, we had some rear grip and we could be competitive.

That first win was a massive relief and in the next round at Motegi I produced what I still consider to be one of the best races of my entire career. We'd qualified third and never really looked like being on the pace in free practice, when Dovizioso had been setting the most consistent times, but it opened up for me on the first lap and I hit the front. We knew that we didn't have the acceleration to get out of the corners and line up a pass on the brakes so once I found myself in front I just pushed as hard as I could and hung on for dear life for the next

twenty-four laps. I knew that bike wasn't capable of winning
that day but I was going for it.

I can honestly say I was pushing the limit on every single
lap, except for maybe the last two when I had a slight gap.
Dovi was right behind me the whole way with Valentino not
much further back and Jorge right behind him and the three
of them didn't let go. I was on the mat every single lap but
I managed not to make a single mistake. I was physically
destroyed at the end because I had put so much effort
in and the next Ducati was so far back it wasn't funny; about
50 seconds behind me in twelfth place.

We finished the season with one more win at Phillip Island,
making it just three for the season but each one of them was
particularly sweet to me because we knew we had done it
against the odds, on a bike that shouldn't really have been
winning. It has taken Valentino Rossi to go to Ducati and fail
for people to realise that maybe I was better than what people
first thought.

Ducati have tried to blame Filippo Preziosi, who designed
the Desmosedici, for their problems but that isn't fair. I believe
that if we had been given the right support at the right time
we could have made a really great bike together. I know it isn't
healthy to contemplate what might have been but sometimes
you can't help it. It wouldn't have taken much to change
things in 2008 and if I'd had no health problems in 2009 and
a good working relationship in 2010 we could have feasibly
won one or even three more championships for Ducati in a

row. And who knows how many more after that? I could have happily stayed at Ducati for the rest of my career before all the speculation and malicious gossip around my illness. The fact I left was their doing, not mine.

I'm at peace with the way everything panned out as it did because I learnt a lot and I also got the opportunity to fulfil another dream: to finally follow in the footsteps of Mick Doohan and ride for the factory Repsol Honda team. Only time would tell how that would turn out.

CHAPTER 11

THE PROMISED LAND

For me the move to Honda was a very big deal because this was the team Mick Doohan won five 500cc motorcycle championships with. Honda Racing Corporation were under new management when Shuhei Nakamoto came to me and said that he saw me as the person to help motivate Honda again. They had not won a championship since 2006, with Nicky Hayden, and not truly dominated a season since Valentino Rossi had left at the end of 2003. To hear that belief after Ducati had doubted me was a very welcome validation, especially from a company as big as Honda. Nakamoto told me that morale was low at Honda and the team spirit that had characterised their success in the past was missing. This was my dream team, to run the same colours as Mick, and to think that I could possibly be the person to take them back to the glory days they had enjoyed with him was a motivation for me.

A move to the Repsol Honda factory team would mean that for the first time I would be sharing a garage with Dani Pedrosa, who I knew would be my most competitive teammate ever. I saw that as a good thing. I've always had a lot of respect for Dani, and his talent on a bike, ever since I saw him for the first time in the Spanish Championship in 2000. Even though his results weren't great back in those early days I can remember saying to my dad at the time that he had a really nice style about him. Of course he went on to become one of the best riders of his era, a 125cc and 250cc World Champion, and we had battled many times in the smaller classes.

Joining Honda also meant we would be working with my old team boss from Ducati, Livio Suppo, but contrary to what a lot of people might think, Livio played no part in our decision to go to Honda. It was just coincidence, and a lot of the reasons I left Ducati were some of the same reasons that Livio left too. I know he wasn't happy that they effectively asked him to work against me in 2009 but thankfully we'd been able to maintain a good relationship. I have a lot of respect for Livio and I was happy to work with him again but the last year had made me cautious with most people in the paddock. I'd learnt the hard way.

Livio: 'I believe Casey would have moved to HRC even if I was not there. HRC is a kind of "dream" for anybody with a passsion for motorcycle racing. For any rider it is something special to race in the Repsol Honda colours, and (especially for Casey) the same colours as Mick Doohan.'

Honda allowed me to bring almost all of my crew over, including my chief engineer Cristian Gabbarini and my mechanics Bruno Leoni, Roberto Clerici, Andrea Brunetti, Filippo Brunetti and Lorenzo Gagni, although unfortunately we had to leave my electronics guy Gabriele 'Bistecca' Conti behind. I desperately wanted Bistecca to join us because he was one of the best crew members I have ever had – he always knew exactly what I wanted without me having to ask – but he had already signed a multi-year contract with Ducati that he couldn't break. I still had a great bunch of guys around me who I trusted and hoped to keep with me for as long as I continued racing.

Honda were prepared to do whatever we wanted to the bike but in reality it was good from the start and we just needed to make minor adjustments to make it suit me. We started off with the 2010 model at Valencia so that I could give them a steer on winter development but the moment I got on, it felt like an incredible machine. I could open the throttle and it turned. It was finishing off the corners for me so I could turn my attention to picking it up and driving it out and in the first part of corner entry it was so stable. We had to work on braking, and the electronics package wasn't quite what we had with the Ducati, but the difference was that the Ducati really needed the electronics. With the Honda we could make do with what we had because the rest of the package was so good.

Shuhei Nakamoto: 'After the Valencia test I realised my rider choice was correct. For sure, Casey is one of the best riders I've worked with. He also helped us to improve the machine, especially the traction control because his control of the throttle was better than the electronics and our engineers had the opportunity to "be inspired" by him.'

It was also a big advantage to me that I was now sharing the garage with somebody who I could cross-reference data with. Dani and I could both test new parts, give our opinions and take the bike forward in a similar direction. With my previous teammates they would be testing things, saying what they liked and didn't like but, to be blunt, they were nowhere near my pace on the Ducati so their opinion wasn't as helpful to me as it could have been. That in turn doesn't help the development of a bike. With Dani that all changed and we were able to work together to benefit both of us and the factory. I could find out his opinion about a chassis or engine characteristic and we had similar views so we found we agreed on which direction Honda should head in.

In the two pre-season tests at Sepang we made our chassis choice for the start of the season, improved the electronics as much as we could and adapted my corner entry points and other references, which were completely different to the Ducati. We continued to make progress in the final pre-season test in Qatar and as well as setting fast times we knew we had a bike that was a much stronger package in a race situation than anything we had before. From riding on eggshells on the

Ducati and finding it difficult to pass with confidence, going to Honda and being able to put the bike almost anywhere I wanted it made it much easier. For the first time I could overtake in short corners with confidence. It was exciting to have such a strong bike.

According to James Strong: 'The first event of a championship season in any sport has an extra sense of anticipation, of excitement and uncertainty. It is the first real test of a new field of competitors after a "break", which everyone knows has been anything but a rest period.'

James was right.

We went fastest at the Qatar test and had our set-up well sorted for the first round of the season, which got under way just a few days later at the same track. We kept our pace going through free practice, set the fastest lap in every session and qualified on pole by a couple of tenths of a second from Dani. We couldn't have been much better prepared for the race and even though I lost positions to Dani and Jorge on the first lap I always felt comfortable.

I sat behind Dani for a while but was completely relaxed in the first part of the race. Once I got in front of Dani I started making a plan to take on Jorge, lining him up through the long sweeping left at turn eleven and then taking the inside into turn twelve, the first of a series of three fast rights that build from about 180km/h to 200km/h. I was able to do it again ten laps later, getting Dani back after he'd passed me on the brakes into turn one at the start of the sixth lap.

Unlike the previous season when I had won in Qatar but headed to Europe feeling sceptical about our chances on the European circuits, I was looking forward to racing at Jerez in round two and taking on the Spanish riders at their home track. There was nothing between Dani and me on the first day of free practice, when we both went inside the circuit record, but I managed to steal pole from him in qualifying even though I wasn't totally happy with the balance of the bike.

On the Sunday it poured with rain. We'd warmed up in the wet so I had an idea of what the conditions would be like for the race. During that warm up, even though the track was wet, there was a lot of degradation on the allocated tyres and I thought they might not last the distance. With that in mind, I started the race well and tried not to push too hard to conserve my tyres in case it rained harder later on and I needed tread left. The wet had brought new confidence to some riders. Conserving tyres like I was meant the riders behind me were able to catch up and they started passing me. They were playing for the short not the long game. I had no problem losing positions that early in the race as I knew it was the last five to eight laps that counted. Unfortunately, Valentino saw an opportunity to pass me and took a big risk considering it was so early in the race.

On the eighth lap as I grabbed the brakes for turn one, the second-hardest braking zone on the track, Valentino tried a move on the inside that could be described as optimistic at best. I wasn't concerned about being passed by him at that point of the race so I gave him plenty of room but there was no way he was going to make the corner and sure enough he lost the front, taking me down with him.

After eventually finishing fifth in a race won by Jorge, with Dani second, Valentino came around to our garage to 'apologise', although the fact he was still wearing his helmet tells you how sincere the gesture was. I made a comment that was picked up by the television cameras that, as he well knew, had followed him into our garage: 'Clearly your ambition outweighed your talent.'

I said it lightly but I meant it. Everybody had built Valentino up to be this great motor racing genius. They thought he was better than everybody else racing against him in the past and it gave him great confidence, which snowballed into further success. Winning became a habit and he drew great strength from that. This is just my opinion but I genuinely feel that if he had come through during a more difficult era, like the one myself, Dani, Jorge, Dovi and Simoncelli came through, he wouldn't have enjoyed the same level of success early in his career and he wouldn't have developed into the same rider as a result.

Of course after Jerez I took another hammering from the press, who accused me of disrespecting a great champion, but I stand firmly by my comment to this day. There was never a truer word said. It doesn't matter about Rossi's past achievements or seeming greatness, at that moment in time his ambition outweighed his talent, simple as that. That is why he crashed instead of making the pass. And of course I was angry, he not only took me down with him, I also lost twenty-five points to my strongest rival in a championship fight he was never going to be a part of.

It is important to me that people realise I always have a lot of respect for all of my competitors, but I can't say that about Valentino because I feel he shows none in return. He rarely accepts when he has been beaten by the better man on the day; if he gets beaten it's because the other rider's bike is better.

The level of respect that Dani, Jorge and myself show for each other is something that's been missing at the top level of the sport for too many years. The first time I beat Valentino in Qatar he rubbed me on the head, congratulated me and all the rest of it. He obviously thought that was a fluke. As soon as I became a fierce competitor everything was different but it wasn't me who changed.

I warned Filippo Preziosi right at the start that signing Valentino was a no-win situation for him. 'If he wins he'll say it's because of him, if he loses he will blame you and the bike,' I told him. Sure enough he lost and Filippo was moved sideways, which makes me sad because I know there was nothing fundamentally wrong with that bike. I think everybody thought Valentino and Jeremy Burgess (JB) were going to develop the bike because they had this reputation after turning the Yamaha around. They peddled this notion that it was not just about them going fast but about developing a bike that everybody could ride, which was a load of rubbish and it was proven so in the two years they tried. Now they speak badly about Ducati not listening to them and seem to be echoing my words. In reality, Ducati did anything and everything they asked for.

To me it has been a very sad episode in Ducati's history. Not only did it destroy their reputation, it also destroyed their brand. Suddenly this stunning blood red that they were so synonymous with, like Ferrari, was covered in luminous yellow. It wasn't good to see that and I was disappointed for the friends I still had there, especially Filippo. Believe me, by letting that man go Ducati have lost a genius.

As strange as this sounds I genuinely wanted Ducati to succeed, for all the people who work there and for the sake of the championship, which needs as many competitive factories running at the front as possible. However, I must admit that from a purely personal point of view it was a sweet feeling to see Valentino and JB struggle because of what everybody had assumed about my development skills and the expectations everyone had of them. JB is a guy who I have tremendous respect for because of what he has achieved in his career but he said some things that disappointed me at the end of 2010, about the Ducati's problems being a simple set-up issue. Somebody of his calibre should have known better than that. He was disrespecting one of their biggest competitors as a rider and an engineer and had not given any respect to what we had been able to achieve before they even worked with the bike. When they got hold of the bike and couldn't get it working they had the cheek to try and blame it on me. I enjoyed watching Valentino struggle on the Ducati, as he'd made it very clear that before that happened he thought the reason for my success was the bike. Even when that bike wasn't working I put it on the podium and they were nowhere near it, unless a bunch of riders crashed or it rained.

———

As far as my championship was concerned after Jerez I knew I had to ride without making any mistakes if I was going to stand a chance of challenging for the title. I was already twenty points shy of Jorge and eleven behind Dani, a gap that extended to twenty-four and twenty after the next round in Portgual. My chances of chasing them for the win at Estoril were ruined on the first lap by Marco Simoncelli – who cut me off in turn one and then crashed right in front of me in turn four – as well as my old back injury from 2003, which flared up again. At some point during that race I felt my back completely lock up on me and I couldn't move for three or four corners. I was struggling to do anything and could hardly breathe so for a moment I thought I would have to pull in but thankfully within half a lap it eased up a little, got better and we managed to finish in third place.

Now in his second season, Simoncelli was quickly emerging as a genuine podium threat at the front of the pack but his aggressive riding was becoming a bit too much for the rest of us. He was a big guy and when he leaned on you it was difficult to move him. After a race with Marco you would both finish up with tyre marks all over your leathers. I was one of the ones to speak my mind against him in the Safety Commission meetings but I also pulled him to one side on the way out and said, 'Look, you are going to be fast and I have loads of respect for you but you just don't need to ride in that way.'

I was concerned, especially because of the support that Marco's tactics were getting amongst the press and the fans, which seemed to overlook the dangers we were all facing. People were being fed the impression that riders are indestructible and any level of contact is fair game. The most shocking thing I heard on the matter came from the Race Director, Paul Butler, who said in an interview at the time that motorcycle racing is a 'contact sport'. What a load of rubbish. Boxing is a contact sport, where fighters must hit each other in order to score points. Rugby is a contact sport, where guys tackle each other as hard as they can in order to recover possession of the ball. Motorcycle racing is NOT a contact sport. Sure, contact can occasionally happen but it is not necessary in order to win and, as a rule, being knocked off a motorbike at 340km/h plus usually has far more serious consequences than being punched in the face by a guy wearing gloves. But even Dorna CEO Carmelo Ezpeleta didn't want to hear about it and he blew up at those of us who were voicing our concerns.

There was a famous press conference before the race at Estoril, when Marco joked that he would have to be arrested because he refused to accept Jorge's insistence that his riding needed to change. His comments got a big laugh from the journalists but two weeks later he cut across Dani at Le Mans, causing him to crash and break his collarbone. This was not Marco's first incident in which he'd caused another rider to crash. Some people had the nerve to suggest Dani could have avoided the collision but when you are already braking so close to the limit, as we are in every corner, you can't just brake harder because somebody tips in in front of you.

By the time Dani went down on the eighteenth lap of that race in France I was already clear at the front by over 3 seconds after an excellent weekend. We'd improved the bike in a post-race test at Estoril and barely had to touch the set-up when we arrived at Le Mans. We went fastest in every session, including the warm-up, and eventually won by over 14 seconds from Dovizioso – the biggest win margin of my MotoGP career in a dry race, which was satisfying considering I had never won there before.

I was fastest again in every free practice session in Barcelona but we had some tyre issues in qualifying and lost out on pole to Marco. (Marco seemed to quieten down after the incident at Le Mans. Barcelona was Dani's home GP and Marco got a lot of abuse for what had happened in the last race. As the

year went on I became more and more impressed by his
riding.) After a brief battle with Jorge over the first four laps
of the race we managed to get into a rhythm that we knew
he wouldn't be able to stick at and made a gap of around
2 seconds that I was able to control until the last few laps,
when Jorge finally backed off.

Because of his injury Dani was missing from that race
and again at Silverstone, where we arrived just seven points
behind Jorge at the top of the championship thanks to those
back-to-back wins at Le Mans and Barcelona. Once again we
managed to set the pace in every session and even though
it poured down on race day we were happy we had a good
setting for the wet. I didn't get the best of starts and had to
wait a couple of laps for the tyres to come up to temperature,
losing positions to Dovi and Jorge, but managed to get back to
the front despite all the spray from the standing water getting
up inside my visor.

I covered my lines for the first five laps or so and once my
visor started to clear I was able to set the times I was looking
for and opened up a bit of a gap. In the meantime Jorge was
trying to get past Dovi and chase me but unfortunately he lost
the rear and had a big highside. It was a tough and cold race
but we held it together for the win, moving from seven points
behind Jorge to eighteen points ahead. Now the pressure was
on him not to make any more mistakes.

From our point of view we were hitting our best form since
2008 and we extended our podium run to six with a second

place at Assen and two thirds at Mugello and Sachsenring, both from pole. We had some set-up and tyre issues in those races but thankfully Jorge only managed to pull a total of three points back on us and we returned to winning ways with one of my best ever races at Laguna Seca.

Again we struggled in practice to get the feeling we wanted from the tyres and changed the set-up quite substantially, moving the swingarm pivot position and trying to get the rear to work with a little less temperature in the tyre. We managed to do that but couldn't get the grip we needed and were struggling with wheelspin on the rear and a lack of feel from the front. Going into the race we were about two-tenths of a second off the pace of Dani and Jorge and our chances did not look too great.

I don't think either of them really expected me to be challenging either but we turned the bike upside down overnight and found something in warm-up that I was a little happier with. The bike still didn't feel that great with a full tank of fuel but I stayed patient, took my time and stayed close enough to the pair of them so that they didn't get too far away. I waited and watched, learning different lines and ways to ride this set-up, feeling my way into the race. I saw Dani start to tire and drop back from Jorge just past mid-race distance, at which point I knew I needed to pass him, which I did at the Corkscrew a couple of laps later.

I'd been watching Jorge, working out where he was better and where I was better and looking for places to pass. There were a couple of spots, like up on the Corkscrew where I had passed Dani, but I was waiting to get a good clean run. One thing about Jorge is that he hardly ever makes a mistake so it was a case of working out where I was stronger than him and trying to take advantage. I had noticed on a couple of occasions that he didn't get the perfect drive out of the last turn and lost his momentum down the straight. I don't know if his wheelie control was cutting in or he was backing off a little bit too much to keep the front down but it was causing him to lose speed as we came towards the crest at turn one.

The scary thing about that part of the track is that you have no idea where the crest is until you go over it. You are short-shifting out of a tight left-hander all the way up to fifth gear, trying so hard to get the power to the track whilst keeping the front down, and then suddenly everything gets light and starts sliding around underneath you at over 265km/h – I always had an absolute ball going over there. I had my bike geared longer for that particular section so that instead of hitting the limiter when the bike went light I was still getting drive. That gave me a crucial opportunity to make up ground on Jorge every lap and after closing the gap from 0.9 seconds to 0.2 seconds he gave me another opportunity to get the run on him in turn one. Instead of backing off and slipping behind him I decided to carry my momentum and squeeze around the outside of him.

It looked dangerous on television and even though there was barely more space than the width of the white line to ride around him and a concrete wall just a few metres to my right, I knew I had the momentum to make it through.

At that point of the race Jorge was running in the low 1 minute 22 seconds, but once I got in front of him I dropped the hammer again and dipped back into the 1 minute 21 seconds, opening up eight-tenths of a second per lap for the next three laps and effectively killing the race off. That was a great win for us, to come back from the problems we'd had in practice and finish so strongly when our rivals least expected it. I'm not sure why they were so surprised because it wasn't the only time we had turned things around overnight and it was down to our approach to practice that allowed us to do it.

I feel that Jorge, Dani, Valentino and most of the other riders work to a methodical system during practice, starting the weekend by gradually getting faster and faster, analysing the data and making a plan of where they are going to get on the throttle, where to brake, et cetera. From there they try to brake a bit later the next time and a bit later again, getting on the throttle earlier and step by step getting closer and closer to the edge. It's a method of ruling things out and gradually finding the limit. The problem is that when they don't get the bike right they can't find that limit and they can't go fast.

To me it is very simple to work out where the braking point is, where I want the bike to go and what I want it to do. Because I have never had a problem learning tracks, adapting to different conditions or riding a bike that wasn't set up right

I was often quicker out of the box on a Friday morning than the other guys. I was always on the edge of grip and no grip, constantly going over the limit and bringing it back, listening to what the bike was telling me. If it wasn't doing what I wanted straight away I'd come back in and change it. It's hard to explain how I could do this exactly but I had developed a feel for a bike and its relationship to speed during my career and it's something I could pick up quickly.

My approach had its downfalls too because it wasn't always the best way to find the ideal set-up. I was able to do things differently with Honda than I'd done with Ducati because with Ducati we hadn't always been able to find the ideal set-up. I learnt to ride around the problems and change my technique to get the most out of the bike. With Honda there was so much more potential because we were able to find a set-up I was happy with and so I didn't have to ride around all the issues. I still didn't need to do long runs, like I was often forced to do when I was at Ducati, because I'd proved that they aren't important. What's important is getting the bike right and then you can move on from there. We stuffed up a couple of times but so has everybody. Unfortunately my mistakes probably stood out more because people could point to the fact we'd only done short runs and blame it on that. Lorenzo, Dani and Rossi have all dropped back in plenty of races because they didn't find a set-up despite clocking up a hundred laps in practice. It has always been my way to focus more on what isn't working and trying to fix it rather than improving what's going well and more often than not we were pretty close to the mark.

That weekend at Laguna I never did a run longer than six laps in practice, whilst Jorge was doing ten- and eleven-lap runs pretty much every time he was out on track. People would often say things like, 'Jorge is a robot, he can keep turning out lap after lap in practice within a tenth.' That's true but if they are not as fast as mine then it doesn't matter if he can do those laps all day long. If I pull a second on him over the first two laps then he's got to try and make that time up over the rest of the race, and if he hasn't shaken me off by the last couple of laps there is every chance I can pull something out of the hat.

Often I would play down my chances after qualifying and if we weren't doing well I deliberately made it sound like we weren't going to be a threat at all. My rivals would go into a race thinking they had us covered but we'd come out on race day with something extra they weren't expecting, which had to have an effect on them mentally. If they thought we could do that when things were going badly then what did they think we could do to them when we were on the pace?

That's exactly what happened in the next round of 2011 at Brno. Dani had looked like he was going to be the man all weekend but the reality was that the only time I felt he was faster than us was in the mornings. Even though he still went quicker than us in the afternoon we knew we had the pace in the heat and I was holding back a little extra. I qualified third behind Dani and Jorge but got to the front on the third lap of the race, at which point Dani crashed. The conditions were a bit warmer than they had been the previous day, with track temperatures up by 7°C, and it seemed that Jorge was struggling to adapt. In the end he dropped back to fourth and I won by over 6 seconds from Dovi, giving us a 32-point lead at the top of the championship.

Adriana was with me at every race and having her there meant a lot. We had settled into married life well and finding out she was pregnant with our first child was one of the best moments of my life. We'd wanted to start a family for a while and were at home in Switzerland when Adri woke up early and did a test.

Adriana: 'It was positive and I woke Casey up straightaway to tell him. We couldn't have been happier. He was so excited he cancelled training for the day so we could celebrate and we had a look in a few baby stores in Lausanne.'

We waited for a few months and then announced the pregnancy that weekend in Brno at the pre-event press conference.

At this point everything was looking up and in the middle of the 2011 season I was able to buy the property where I had first learnt to ride a motorbike. It had been my dream to own this land since I was a child so it meant a lot. To get to this point was really something, considering only a few years before we'd been living on hand-to-mouth deals in the 125cc and 250cc classes.

I have lived in many, many places since I left Niangala as a four-year-old boy but as I have said, something about that place had gripped me and never let go. The road up there winds from around 300 metres above sea level up to over 1100 metres in just 5 kilometres, so the difference in atmosphere is quite dramatic and the conditions can be really changeable. It can be 30°C and sunny for days on end and then you wake up the next day and it's 10°C and misty. You can open the curtains one morning in winter and the whole place is covered in snow and when the thunderstorms come in, as they regularly do, the whole house shakes and the windows rattle. There's nothing quite like sitting on the front verandah listening to the rain bouncing off the tin roof and watching the light show over the hills around me.

The basic bike skills I'd learnt on that land helped me, over twenty years later, to be where I was in the World Championship. I travelled back to race at Indianapolis in late August and we took our third win in a row and our tenth consecutive podium. Like Laguna Seca, Indy was a circuit where nobody had much experience and there was never much grip, circumstances I loved, even though I had never had a lot of luck there in the past – my first race there in 2008 had been cut short by Hurricane Ike, I missed out in 2009 because of my illness and I'd crashed in 2010. I almost went down again this time when I closed the front a few laps into the race but I managed to save it with my knee and put in a few good lap times that pulled a big enough gap on Dani to win with a little to spare.

Our seventh victory of the season gave us a 44-point advantage that we managed to maintain with a third place at

Misano. I struggled a bit with a neck injury I'd picked up in a crash during practice earlier in the season at Assen but rode through it and then scored another win at Aragon. With three races to go we knew that victory in the next round at Motegi would leave us needing to score just one point more than Jorge to wrap up the championship at Phillip Island, a dream scenario at my home track.

I flew to Japan on my own because we didn't want to take any risks with Adri's health or the health of our unborn baby. After the devastating March tsunami had damaged the nuclear plant in Fukushima there was ongoing media reports about radiation leaks and Motegi was only about 100 kilometres from there. It was strange not having Adriana at the race but on track everything started perfectly. We took our tenth pole position of the season with a new lap record in qualifying and I managed to pull a second on Dovi over the opening three laps of the race. Then on the fourth lap, as I came onto the back straight my bike started pumping, which shook the brake pads out from the disc. As I hit my braking point the lever immediately hit the bar as there were no brakes there. I pumped the brakes as quickly as I could to get them back and they returned so fast they almost put me over the front of the bike. By the time all that happened I'd missed my braking point and I ran wide and off the circuit. I managed to stay on and get the thing stopped before we hit the wall at the end of the gravel trap but our chance to win was gone. I came back on track in seventh place and managed to work my way back up to third by the end but we were disappointed because we knew we had the bike to win that day.

Now I would have to outscore Jorge by ten points at Phillip Island to win the championship, which made it nothing more than a slim chance. Actually, that wasn't such a bad thing because it relieved the pressure a little bit. I didn't think I could realistically win the championship there so all I was focused on was taking my fifth win in a row at Phillip Island; that was the only pressure I put on myself. Since winning it for the first time in 2007 the expectation amongst the fans and the press had risen every year. After I'd won it twice it was like, 'Can he make it a hat-trick?' Then it was four and now it was five. Of course that's what I wanted but I knew Marco was fast around there, Dani and Dovi too, not to mention Jorge fighting to keep his championship alive.

On the morning of the race things suddenly turned around and I had the opportunity to win the title after all, but not in the way I expected or wanted. Coming out of the final turn at the end of warm-up Jorge lost the rear and had a low side, got his hand trapped under the bike and lost the tip of his finger. I immediately went to visit him in the circuit medical centre and he told me that he wasn't fit to ride and wished me luck for the race. That is the sign of a good person, and the respect I talked about earlier. I never wanted something like this to happen to a rival, especially someone I respected so much, but it was my job to go on and try to win the championship.

I got a good start, opened a gap and for a while I was

cruising. It seemed like nothing could go wrong but then I ran into a wall of rain at turn twelve and the rear stepped out, almost causing me to go down. Suddenly there were people going down everywhere and it became a mission just to stay up and make it to the finish. I was lucky, no doubt about it, but we made the flag to secure my second World Championship and Honda's sixtieth Constructors' Championship with my fifth straight win at Phillip Island – at my home Grand Prix and all on my twenty-sixth birthday! I don't think I could ask for much more than that.

That evening HRC organised a small private party for me and the team in Cowes, the main town on Phillip Island. It was good for me to see the team celebrate and I felt really proud to have been able to come through and give them this. It was a very special moment for me but winning the championship hadn't really sunk in yet. We got back to the hotel room and I couldn't get to sleep; I just lay there thinking about it. After a few hours it was like I was suddenly struck by lightning and that's when it really sunk in, what I had achieved that day.

Up to that season my whole career had been spent with Italian teams – even KTM, which is an Austrian factory but an Italian team – so this was my first time working with the Japanese and I had loved every minute. First of all, they have a very high regard for respect, which they gave to me and I gave back. They also have a great sense of humour and all the Japanese team members and management had quirky characters, so I had a ball with them. The nicest thing was that they made my wins feel so much more important than any other team I had been with. I could see the happiness on their faces and they couldn't have been more grateful to me for the part I had played in our joint success.

I have to say that I feel there is a lack of respect in general towards the Japanese in the paddock from the Europeans. I had heard so many bad things about working for Honda; that Ducati is a family and HRC is a big, heartless corporation but the truth is exactly the reverse. Everybody at Honda puts their heart and soul into the bike and they put themselves under massive pressure to get results, so the relief amongst them when we won that championship was huge.

Looking back on that incredible weekend at Phillip Island there is one other special memory that sticks out, which is that I got to share the podium with Marco Simoncelli. Losing him a week later in such tragic circumstances in Malaysia was a devastating moment for anybody involved in our sport but especially for his family and his girlfriend, Kate. My heart goes out to them every time I think about what happened.

Obviously I'd had my issues with Marco earlier that season, as most of us had, but as the year had gone on he had definitely grown and learnt a lot. It's funny how the little things stick in your mind but I remember being at Misano and I needed a haircut. Marco and Kate had their motorhome parked next to ours so we ended up speaking to them a little bit and Kate organised for a local hairdresser to come onto the track for us. Kate is a really lovely girl, and Marco was a nice guy. He

just needed to calm down and by the end of the season he had
done that – he was riding really well, getting better results as
a consequence and I was not scared to ride with him like I
had been at the start of the season. He was still making hard
passes but there was no contact and I had no complaints about
his style of riding anymore.

In a way, this made Marco's death even harder to take. He
had the talent to win races for sure and in theory the switch back
to 1000cc in 2012 would have favoured him because he was a
bigger guy. Who knows if he could have won championships? If
he could have stepped it up another level again? It would have
been entertaining to watch him try, that's for sure. Tragically
we will never know what his full potential could have been.

Marco's death shocked everyone but it seemed to me that
by the time the 2012 season started up it had been forgotten
too quickly. The most fitting tribute to his memory shouldn't
have been a plaque by the side of the track where he lost his
life, but a real change in the way riders respect each other
and respect the limits. Unfortunately, I don't feel that this
happened. I have always been very aware of what can happen
in this sport, which is why I have always shown respect to my
fellow racers. You might not like the person next to you on
the grid but you have to be aware that if an accident happens,
anyone can be hurt or killed.

Sometimes young riders are so desperate to win that they
forget what's most important. They get built up so much that
they start to believe the hype, they feel invincible. Nobody

is, especially in bike racing. And if a rider doesn't care about his own safety then it stands to reason he doesn't care about anybody else's either. Don't get me wrong, MotoGP is as safe as it has ever been in terms of the gravel traps, circuit layouts and rider equipment, but the fact that certain riders were still putting others at risk even after Marco's death bothered me a lot. It seemed to me that the race organisers still wanted to see biff and barge and Marco's death hadn't changed their perspective. Even the Safety Commission, set up by the riders, seemed to have become less about safety and, for a few members, more about guys trying to get their own way. As far as I was concerned we were basically puppets in a show and I wasn't sure I wanted to be a part of it anymore.

For a few years I'd been feeling differently about the sport I loved. I'd thought I was working with people who shared the same passions and goals as I did but I'd come to realise that wasn't always the case. To be wholly focused on the business of racing and have an eye always on the money wasn't what I was about but more and more I became aware that this was what mattered too often to others. Marco's death wasn't the cause of my disillusionment, but it did bring it all into sharp focus for me. My eyes were open to the negative aspects of MotoGP and I didn't know how to change things.

Before the 2012 season started something far more important than racing motorcycles happened and, suddenly, a decision that I had been considering for a long time became more and more clear and certain in my mind.

CHAPTER 12

GONE FISHING

After so many years focusing on motor racing and the demands of competing as a factory-contracted MotoGP rider, everyone told us that things were about to change dramatically for me and Adri when our baby was born. We couldn't wait but our baby didn't seem in a rush to meet us. Adri had been due to give birth on Sunday, 12 February 2012, but that day came and went without anything happening. After a couple of days, which seemed to me the longest wait ever and so must have felt like weeks for Adri, the doctor told us he wasn't happy with progress. It was worrying when he said that and we ended up at the hospital. Finally at 10 pm on Thursday 16 February our little girl, Alessandra Maria, arrived into the world, weighing in at 2.8 kilograms.

Thankfully, after the delay, everything went to plan and there was no real drama. I didn't like seeing Adri in pain but I've never met a tougher girl than her, she just deals with everything and, of course, Ally came out just perfect. For me it was a strange feeling because everybody tells you all these emotions will hit you when you become a parent so I was waiting for it but it didn't happen straight away. Adri and I took it in our stride. Day by day though, the bond between us and Ally has become stronger and stronger and stronger. It gets to the point where you don't know how your heart can expand much more but somehow it does.

Becoming parents changed the shape of our life to a certain degree but it felt very natural to us both. I can see how it would be a shock to the system for people who like to go out and party all the time but that's not us so the reality of how we live didn't change that much at all; the biggest difference now is that we really have a purpose. Even though travelling is a bit more complicated, I can pretty much do everything I was doing before Ally was born and as soon as she is old enough to come fishing with me I literally won't have to change a thing!

Seriously though, if anything, I think having a child gave us both extra energy. Of course Adri has had times when she has been tired and Ally has struggled with teething or things like this and kept us both up but you battle through. You may wake up at five in the morning because she's patting you on the face but I can't think of a better way to wake up than that – I don't care what time it is! Nowadays every single decision I make is done with Ally and Adri at the forefront of my mind.

But in 2012 I was still racing, it is what I do, so we kept travelling. Ally was born in between the two annual pre-season tests at Sepang which, unlike Ally's birth, were beset by problems. The new RC213V was fantastic but I couldn't even ride it on the first day of the test because of my old back injury, which flared up again when I was warming up. I must have been stretching for a good twenty minutes and then all of a sudden my back just locked up on me. I couldn't move or do anything – I had to call someone to come and help me move into a position that was less painful. We lost another day at the second test because of an engine failure on one of Dani's bikes, which the engineers wanted to fully check out before they allowed either of us back out.

One of the major factors that affected our preparation was the last-minute additional bike weight change – implemented by Dorna. We had to incorporate this onto our bike, which Honda had spent a fortune on designing in the winter. Making those changes disrupted and upset the balance. We spent a lot of time trying to move this additional weight around but it really was a problem. The other big factor we were dealing with was the new specification of tyres provided by Bridgestone. They'd come up with an innovative compound designed to improve warm-up time in response to a bunch of guys crashing on cold tyres during 2011. The feedback from pretty much every other factory about the new rubber was good but for whatever reason on the Honda it gave us unbelievable chatter. We tried everything to solve it, shortening the wheelbase, changing the chassis stiffness and moving the weight around to try and reduce the frequency but nothing worked.

It was a crazy situation because we shouldn't have had to change the bike at all just for the sake of making it suit a specific tyre but this was one of the side effects of the championship switching to a single supplier back in 2008. Bridgestone had won the contract, which you may think I would have been happy about given my history with Michelin, but the truth was quite the opposite. Clearly there was a need for regulation but to me competition amongst the tyre brands is just as important as having different motorcycle factories and different riders on the grid. Having a mix of tyre brands had thrown up some of the most exciting and memorable races in the history of the championship, such as Simon Crafar's win on Dunlops at Donington Park in 1998 or when Makoto Tamada won a bunch of races with Bridgestone in 2004. As far as I am concerned if you're going to give people the same tyres, why not just give everybody the same engine too?

There was another big change to MotoGP at the start of 2012 that really upset me, as a purist and a fan of Grand Prix racing, which was the introduction of 'Claiming Rule Teams' (CRT). CRT (so called because the teams 'claim' ownership of the bikes instead of leasing them from the factories) is basically an excuse to let non-prototype bikes onto the grid just to fill up spaces. It also has the effect of taking Honda,

Ducati and Yamaha's power away from them and giving control over the championship to Carmelo Ezpeleta, just like Bernie Ecclestone has in Formula 1. The difference is that Formula 1 cars are still prototypes, incredible machines, but these new CRT bikes are completely going against what MotoGP is about. There already exists another World Championship for that kind of class.

The way the rules are going, with the standardisation of the remaining prototypes, in a couple of years' time everybody will effectively be on a CRT bike and that is not for me. My dream was to be 500cc World Champion, not the CRT World Champion and it angered me that the 'winning' CRT rider at each race in 2012 would get to join the top three finishers in parc fermé at the end of the race. That exclusive area is supposed to be a privilege for the podium guys only, the realisation of a dream and the reward for a lot of sacrifice and hard work. I know it's tough for those guys who haven't got the opportunity to ride a factory bike but I'm afraid that's life. I was there once too.

I'm pretty sure Carmelo would never have taken such drastic measures if they'd left the rules alone when MotoGP first changed to 990cc four-strokes back in 2002. The goalposts have been moved pretty much every season since then but the decision to go to 800cc in 2007 was particularly ludicrous. It didn't make any sense from a technical perspective because nobody builds 800cc road bikes and it was far more dangerous for the riders. The 1000s are slightly heavier than the 800s and have more straight-line speed so you have to brake earlier and can't carry the same corner speed.

It seems to me that Carmelo made changes because he wanted to be seen making changes like F1. Formula 1 has had to make technical changes to help make their sport more interesting, it was becoming a procession. In motorbike racing you don't need to make changes to create great racing. All they did was generate false hope that the sport would be more appealing. In reality, every time they changed the rules the racing suffered because the factories had to produce a new bike from scratch, which requires millions and millions of dollars of research and development money, which not everybody has. We ended up losing Suzuki and Kawasaki for those very reasons but I'm sure if they had left it at 1000cc from the start those factories would still be around, with the addition of some others like Aprilia or BMW.

Eventually they realised their mistake and moved back to 1000cc in 2012 but for some it was too late, particularly for people like Kenny Roberts, whose project in 2006 was ideal: a factory-spec Honda MotoGP engine in a bespoke chassis made independently by his team. It was a competitive package and Kenny Junior perhaps should have won a race on it before they were forced to shut down their operation due to the rising costs of switching to 800cc. What would we give for a CRT bike like that now?

I'm not saying I have all the answers, not by any means, but reducing electronics would definitely be an easy way to save costs. Complex systems like anti-wheelie and traction control not only take the fun out of riding the bikes but the research and development requires massive investment, not to mention the extra staff each team needs to manage them at the track.

All of these things were playing on my mind when the season started in Qatar, where I was effectively only racing against ten other Grand Prix bikes even though there were supposedly twenty-one on the grid. I finished third in that race despite arm pump problems and managed to win at Jerez but again had arm pump issues and was still having problems with the new tyres so I didn't enjoy a single lap of either of those races. Honda knew that I wasn't enjoying myself and I told them as much when we opened discussions about a new contract for 2013. As always I was completely open and honest with them and I made it clear that I was thinking about walking away from the sport altogether.

In the end they came up with an incredible proposal: a one-year contract that would have pretty much doubled my earnings. It was a crazy offer and it was extremely tempting. Money had never been the lure for me but things had changed and I thought about what it could do for Ally and, if we are lucky enough, any children we might have in the future. It would mean that they would be financially secure for the rest of their lives. Adriana was fantastic; she kept assuring me that our children would be fine, that we were already in the fortunate position of not having to worry about money as long as we looked after what we already had so I didn't have to do anything that my heart wasn't in. I still couldn't make up my mind but I didn't think I could turn my back on the financial freedom it would bring us. I was going to accept. I figured that the competitive side of my nature would provide enough motivation for me to keep going for another year but it meant for the first time in my life I would race purely for the money, something I said I would never do.

I hinted to the team that I was ready to sign but the more I thought about it the less certain I was. Deep down I knew all the reasons why I felt that way kept overpowering the lure of financial gain.

In the week leading up to the race at Estoril a story was published in a Spanish magazine declaring that I was planning to retire, which I denied in the pre-event press conference in Portugal. I was as honest with the press as I had been with Honda because the truth was that I still hadn't made a decision. It is hard not to believe information was leaked, in the hope it would put pressure on me to sign. I know it wasn't Nakamoto-san. I trust him and it's not his style, but I'm pretty sure someone was talking.

Still, as I had done so many times during my career, I put all that media attention to one side for the race and at Estoril I produced one of the best performances of my career, right up there with Motegi 2010 and Laguna Seca 2011, to beat Jorge at one of his favourite tracks. It was a similar race to Motegi, in that I got myself to the front early in the race and just hung on. The difference this time was that even though I was struggling a little with arm pump at the end of the race I knew I had something in reserve if Jorge stepped up the pace.

That win completed a full house of victories at every track I had ever raced at in MotoGP and immediately afterwards I started to feel more convinced that it was the right time to announce my retirement. I continued to think long and hard about it for the rest of that week and on the Monday before the next race at Le Mans I finally made my mind up. Adri knew straight away and I called Mum and Dad then immediately sat down at my computer, sent Nakamoto-san an email and that was it.

As soon as that decision was made I wanted to announce it quickly, for myself and for the team. If I had kept them hanging on until the end of the season and then walked, it wouldn't have been fair because they would have had less time to work on new sponsorship deals and on choosing their new rider. From my perspective it was important for me to tell people so they understood my reasons and knew that I was retiring on my own terms – not because of injury, lack of form or whatever. Coming on the back of those consecutive wins at Jerez and Estoril, the timing could not have been better.

On arrival at Le Mans I called Rhys Edwards, who looks after the team's communications and all my interactions with the media, and asked him to come to my motorhome. 'You're going to retire today, aren't you?' he asked. I nodded. We sat and spoke for about an hour about the best way to explain that I was making the announcement early in the season out of my respect for Honda. Rhys spoke to Livio and Nakamoto-san and we decided to make the announcement at Dorna's regular pre-event press conference that afternoon, which I was invited to already as the current championship leader.

We arranged with Dorna's media staff for me to say a few words before the usual questions to myself and the other riders. As what seemed like a thousand flashbulbs went off in my face I announced that this season would be my last, that there were changes happening in the sport that I wasn't happy with and that I would be finishing at the end of the year to pursue different things in my life. After that I went straight back to our motorhome and it felt a little strange, but at the same time it was a huge relief. I have never felt like I'd made the wrong choice, it sat well with me immediately.

Shuhei Nakamoto: 'Casey's unbelievable performance since the beginning of his two years with us was a great motivation for all Honda Repsol staff, who worked even harder to provide him the best bike possible. He has not the easiest character in the world but he is very honest and I am sure he never lied to me.'

Many in the press labelled me a liar for denying their earlier story. It was disappointing, because I had been frank with them all along but despite my best intentions this approach always seemed to end up earning me a bad rap. Other people

prefer to play games and make up stories but to me it has
always been plain and simple: say it straight so people will
understand what you mean. It took me a while to learn that no
matter how straight you say it there are people in the media
who are only too happy to twist your words according to their
agenda.

Once it was done it was a huge weight off my shoulders
and I felt I could concentrate solely on my racing again. We
still had fifteen races left and I desperately wanted to win the
championship for Honda, for the team and for myself. My
commitment was never in doubt because apart from anything
else I was still very much focused on improving myself as a
rider. Even though I wouldn't say I had a particular weak spot
there was still room for improvement in every aspect of my
riding and that desire to fine tune it had never faded.

The other thing we had to try to master was this chatter
issue, which we continued to ride around pretty much every
weekend. There was the odd race when it wasn't an issue but
we weren't able to capitalise, such as Germany. For whatever
reason the chatter wasn't so bad in left-hand corners and with
Sachsenring being an anti-clockwise track Dani and I were
able to completely dominate. We were miles out in front on
the last lap and I felt I had plenty of speed to pass Dani on the
last corner so I went wide on the second to last corner to line
him up and get a better exit. Unfortunately I tucked the front.

It was frustrating when Dani beat us because he was
my teammate but I didn't feel any jealousy towards him.

It annoyed me that he'd got the bike working when we couldn't but it was the same for him when it was the other way around. Some days he beat us but to be honest I always felt like I had the measure of him over the course of a season. I think over the years the only teammate I didn't have the measure of was David Checa in my first year in 250cc and back then I was still learning. I never felt threatened by a teammate because I have never had one that I felt was consistently quicker than me and throughout my career our biggest competition always came from outside the garage. Still, I have great respect for Dani, our partnership was a fruitful one and I think we worked really well together to help Honda build their best ever bike in the RC213V.

Dani had started using a new chassis from the Mugello test a few weeks earlier but to me it was no better so I'd stuck with the old one. The feel was slightly different and I think Dani preferred it just a little bit, but I didn't believe either of us could go any quicker with it and it didn't solve the chatter problem. To a lot of people it seemed the new chassis had turned Dani's season around but if you look at the results he didn't start winning regularly until Indianapolis, which also happened to be the weekend that my championship ended.

We'd had a few problems with the electronics on the Friday at Indy and also had a stone get caught in the chain, which cost us track time, but I set the pace on Saturday morning and I really felt we had the speed to dominate the race. Despite all our problems that season we had still gone there with a possibility of winning the championship, thanks to further wins at Assen and Laguna, that left us only thirty-two points behind Jorge with eight races still to go. Everything changed within a split second on the fourth lap of qualifying, when the rear stepped out on the exit of the left-hand turn thirteen and launched me over the front of the bike at around 150km/h.

The first thing to touch the ground was the toe of my boot and the impact ripped my foot around. Imagine driving along in your car at that speed and sticking your foot out of the door – that's pretty much what it was like. I came down heavily on my front, slid for around 50 metres along the tarmac before rolling across the grass and eventually coming to a stop in the gravel. I looked down at my foot, which was facing sideways, and I remember thinking, This isn't good! Then, as I moved my weight onto my other leg, I felt a pop in my ankle and there was a loud crack. The pain was unreal, so bad that I honestly thought my tibia had come out through the side of my leg. But it was actually the sound of the joint going back into the socket.

I went for scans at a hospital in downtown Indianapolis, where the doctors told me that they'd never seen bone that badly bruised before without it being broken in half – it was so bad that there was bruising to the actual bone marrow. We emailed the American doctor's notes to Dr Neil Halpin in Australia along with a photograph of the ankle, which had ballooned to double its normal size, and I had a short conversation on the phone with him. Dr Halpin told me that he couldn't make a full assessment without seeing the original scan documents, a process that would take several days, but his advice was that I shouldn't race.

Several days was too long for me and we had to make our decision the next morning. Even though I was in a lot of pain I decided to take some painkillers and get on with it. The ankle was so swollen that Alpinestars helped customise a boot two sizes larger than my normal ones to fit me for the race. Thankfully my qualifying time after those three laps was still good enough for sixth on the grid, which gave us a chance of fighting for some decent points, but after a rough start we ended up back in eighth on the first lap and had to fight back.

I was doing that and just as I was closing in on the top four Ben Spies had an engine failure and I found myself in the middle of the smoke, unsure where I was going and what I might hit and I lost a couple of positions again. We fought back up to third place and I was hanging on with seven laps left but the painkillers had gradually worn off. I was compensating for my injury with the other side of my body and it took a toll. I simply had no energy left. It was frustrating to have to give up the final podium position to Dovizioso but at least we knew we had done everything we could and taken some points, which we hoped would keep us in the championship.

Dr Halpin probably wasn't too surprised when he learnt I was going to race: 'Even though I hadn't seen the scans properly yet I could see there was a definite risk of vascular problems, such as a blood clot, which is why my advice was not to race. I have had to push an ankle joint back in for a rugby player before and there was a lot of screaming. Casey's courage is quite extraordinary and I think because he is physically so little you don't expect it. He has an extraordinarily high pain threshold. I have been a professional rugby league doctor at the Sydney Roosters and the Newcastle Knights for over thirty years. I've treated four broken necks, a cardiac arrest, ruptured spleens, all sorts, but Casey is as tough as anybody I have ever met. To get back up with those injuries and race again the next day is one of the toughest things I've seen in sport, up there with Andrew Johns playing in the 1997 Rugby League Grand Final with a broken rib and partly collapsed lung. It is also one of the most unwise things I've ever seen too! But ultimately as a doctor all you can do is give advice. The decision is up to the patient.'

Blocking pain out is something my mum taught me to do when I was very small. Her method was quite unusual but it worked: she used to tickle me. It was something she had learnt as a little girl from being constantly tickled by her older siblings. Eventually she realised that through the power of mind over matter she could block it out and not react. She later applied the same theory to physical pain and through tickling me taught me how. Even though I am clearly not immune to pain I am able to put it to one side when I really have to.

After the race we sent the original scans back to Australia by courier so that Dr Halpin could properly analyse them but it was an anxious wait for the results. The next race was the following weekend in the Czech Republic so we had no alternative but to travel from the USA to Europe and hope for the best. To be honest, having already raced at Indy, I fully expected to be competing again at Brno but the day before free practice was due to start the news came through: I needed immediate surgery and would have to miss the next three races at least, maybe even the rest of the season. Either way, our championship was over.

Dr Neil Halpin: 'Casey flew to the Czech Republic and I thought, You're crazy, you're not going to make it! I studied the plates and I could see he had five fractures inside his ankle. He had a 10-millimetre fracture to the talus bone, which is the ball of the ankle joint, a fracture at the bottom end of the tibia and torn multiple ligaments including the deltoid ligament, which is the main ligament complex on the inside of the ankle. Thankfully Casey decided to follow my advice and flew back to Australia to have surgery. I saw him on 27 August and we did an arthroscopic procedure on the thirtieth.'

I'd had to wait three days for the operation after seeing Dr Halpin because they needed the swelling to go down first, otherwise I would have had the surgery immediately. The period after the surgery was frustrating but there was nothing I could do about it. Knowing that I had no chance to retire as World Champion I started focusing on my recovery for Phillip Island, which was two months away. Winning there for the sixth time in a row would at least be a nice way to sign off from my career and give myself some kind of closure on everything that had happened that year. I spent six weeks recovering. (While I was having trouble walking, Ally was mastering getting around in a walker. She would occasionally launch herself at me and bash into my ankle on the way. Probably not the best way to give the ankle a rest but I wasn't about to stop her!) We were able to come back as planned for the Japanese round at Motegi, which along with the next round at Sepang would give me a chance to get a feel for the bike and test my fitness before my home Grand Prix. I hadn't trained in months and could still barely walk on my ankle but just like when I came back from illness in 2009 I didn't believe it was going to be a problem. I knew that my body would pull through if I needed it.

We managed fifth place in Japan, where I struggled to get the bike fully leaned over because I couldn't get my foot out of the way. Sepang was less physically demanding, firstly because there aren't so many slow corners that I needed to pick the bike up from and also because it rained on race day. There was more of a risk of crashing, of course, which would have been a complete disaster but we stuck it out and got our reward with a podium. That set us up nicely for Phillip Island.

This was a big race that meant a lot. As always Adri was there, she gave me a kiss on the front of my crash helmet before heading back to the garage as the rest of the grid was cleared.

As soon as the lights went out I released the clutch but I was a split second too late and Lorenzo and Dani both made the jump and edged ahead of me on the inside.

The key to the start is not to be overly committed. If you are committed to one line then you are going to cut people up and that's no good for them or you so, especially over the last few years of my career, I have learnt to go into the first turn of the race with caution. I have always prided myself on the fact that I have never taken another rider out in any part of the race, apart from Sete Gibernau at Estoril in 2006. But I have never gone punching in and knocked somebody off the track. I'll even apologise if I get too close.

We were safely tucked into third position ahead of the two satellite Yamahas of Cal Crutchlow and Andrea Dovizioso as we came into the long left-hander at turn two, Doohan Corner.

Turn three at Phillip Island is a fast downhill left-hander, almost flat out in fifth gear, and it is probably my favourite corner in the world. Unbelievably, it is now also named after me. There was a ceremony the Thursday before the race and I was given a commemorative plate with twenty-seven diamonds in it, to match my racing number, which was something quite special. It is a great privilege and pretty cool to have a corner named after you, but especially so because apparently I ride this corner differently to anybody else.

I can particularly remember my qualifying lap here in 2011. With new tyres and loads of grip I went into turn three and shut off for the least amount of time I ever have and then got straight back on the throttle. The data showed I was at 262km/h and the slowest point of the corner was 258km/h. It was damn quick but I was completely sideways and had my front wheel halfway across the kerb. That day I got it as good as I ever have but every time I go through this corner it gives me a great rush and really gets the blood flowing. This time was no different.

Dani Pedrosa needed to win this race to have any realistic chance of keeping his title hopes alive. He was fighting hard, attacking from the front, and he got the best of Jorge at turn four, Honda Corner – a tight right-hand hairpin – to take the lead, forcing Jorge to sit up.

I knew I had the pace to win so I wasn't worried about being in third on the first lap. I knew I could afford to be patient, hold back and pick my moment. We were making ground on almost every corner and as we came around the long sweeping left-hand turn eleven to complete the lap I drove up the inside of Jorge coming out of the last corner. Dani was immediately ahead of me as we tipped into Doohan Corner for the second time, peeled around turn two and then slid into Stoner Corner. (It still sounds weird to call it that.)

When Dani turned into turn four, he ran a little wide and as the circuit was deteriorating out wider when he tried to get back for the apex he lost the front on the rough tarmac, spinning him across the bitumen and ending his championship. I felt for him – it's a small mistake that's very easy to make but the bottom line was I now had clear track ahead of me. Jorge knew that second place was enough for him to wrap up the title and even though he was desperate to celebrate with a win I knew he wouldn't take as many risks. All I had to do was stick to my pace, stay focused and make the most of the opportunity.

I always used to enjoy riding my Ducati at Phillip Island, it is one of the best tracks in the world for that bike. It had quite a long wheelbase so it was stable in the long fast corners. It would move a little but it had a stability that the Honda doesn't have, it can get a little nervous and twitchy if the set-up isn't right so we have really had to work hard to get comfortable with it. But once we found what we were looking for it became a lot easier.

I had just twenty-five laps of the track left to go riding the fastest motorcycle ever built.

After twelve laps I had a 4-second advantage over Jorge but I let it drop slightly, allowing him to close the gap before pushing to open it up again, purely for the sake of giving myself an extra point of focus. You only have to lose your concentration for a split second before you end up like Dani did in turn four. The only thing I allow to distract me is the crowd. There were Australian flags everywhere and I wanted to soak up this unique moment in my life. The final two laps were the best. I knew the race was wrapped up and I didn't have to look after the tyres anymore. I spun the rear tyre even more than I needed to through turn three and enjoyed the corner.

After twenty-seven laps – the perfect number – I came out of turn twelve for the final time and saw the chequered flag being prepared. It's a familiar moment of relief and joy but that day it held extra significance. Winning at Phillip Island for the sixth time was the perfect way to finish my MotoGP career.

The celebrations after the race were awesome and everywhere I turned someone wanted to congratulate me or shake my hand. Adri, Ally, Mum, Dad and lots of friends were there to share it all with me and that made it even more special. It was a great way to say goodbye to the sport and celebrate all we'd achieved.

While putting this book together Livio sent this message to be included: 'Working with Casey has been something very special. He has, as a person, all the quality values (honesty, love of family, respect for the people he works with) and as a rider, he is simply "the fastest man on earth", by far. His talent is unbelievable. There are some moments in his career that I will never forget. His first test at Qatar, under artificial lights was so much faster than the others that I thought he'd found a short cut.'

Earning the respect of people like Livio and the team means a lot to me and the friendships I've made through racing have given me and my family so much more than I'd ever dreamed of. I was leaving at the right time but stepping away from competition did mean people I'd spent so much time with wouldn't be part of my day-to-day life any longer. Saying goodbye is always hard.

After the emotional few days at Phillip Island we finished the 2012 Championship with another podium in mixed conditions at Valencia, a race I wanted to win purely to end up with the same number of wins for the season as Dani and Jorge. Considering the races we'd missed, it's pretty incredible that we could have done that. Obviously the year didn't work out how we'd hoped and I was happy for Jorge, who fully deserved his championship, but without the chatter problems early in the year and the ankle injury I know that Dani and I could have dominated that season even more, without a doubt.

I learnt a lot in those last two years of my MotoGP career, about myself, my priorities and my life in general. Throughout my career, racing was always my sole focus and I thought I had to do it all on my own. I'd seen other riders with heaps of people around them – a personal assistant, public relations person, etc. – but I never felt like I needed that. I was wrong. When I started working with Honda press officer Rhys Edwards, he helped show me that I didn't have to be so serious about it all, or take it all on my shoulders. He knows perfectly where the line is and when you can get away with light-hearted fun and when it's time to be all business.

I like Rhys's attitude, he always has a joke handy and can defuse an awkward situation (or occasionally cause one!) when needed.

With Rhys and my close friend Chris Hillard from Alpinestars around I started to enjoy myself at the track a lot more. Adri and Ally were also a big part of me getting my head away from bikes. It is healthy to have other interests and it had an added benefit too, because I was building up my physical and psychological reserves without even realising it. Up until the last few years I'd pushed so hard all the time that my tank was always on the red line, so as soon as illness or anything stressful happened I was instantly eating into my reserves. It is probably not surprising that eventually I felt burnt out. It wasn't until I had achieved my goals in the sport that I felt I could start to enjoy other things in life.

I needed to get away and relax a little, and that's something I am making a conscious effort to do now that I am starting my next adventure. I've learnt it's really important to keep a balance in your life and make sure you don't make the highs too high and the lows too low.

Whatever challenges I take on now I am still driven by the same quest to improve – I can't change who I am. As a personality trait this is both a good thing and a bad thing. I like that part of me but it would be nice to not be like that sometimes, to enjoy something without being obsessed with getting better at it. I am sure you can go through life a lot happier if you don't analyse everything. For the time being

I can't see myself changing, though, and that is why I was so quick to set myself new goals.

People say I am going to miss MotoGP and that one day I'll come back but I'm not sure. At the moment I think not. Bikes are still my passion but now I can ride for pure pleasure. There are so many other things I want to do. I am enjoying learning the intricacies of V8s and not really worried about results, though my competitive side always wants more. I want to improve my skiing and snowboarding to the point where I can heli-ski anywhere in the world. Something like that would have been too dangerous for me to try while I was racing bikes for fear of injury, but now I can have a go. My other big passion, besides my family, is fishing, which is something I have done ever since I was a toddler catching trout in the creek up at Niangala. I've always loved it and whenever I was home I would try my luck, even though I didn't really know what I was doing. Now it has turned into a whole different thing.

It was in 2008 that I finally had a bit of time to actually go on a holiday and pursue a hobby that interested me, so I went up north catching barramundi with my cousin Mark and Leon Camier and guided by Jason Wilhelm. I remember we struggled a lot because the conditions weren't good but we kept trying, doing long days and just learning and learning.

At the beginning of 2011 I was introduced to Paul Worsteling, who many people in Australia will know as the fishing expert and host of the television program *IFISH*.

A mutual friend put us in touch and Paul invited me out to Western Australia to fish with him and film a few episodes for his show. I was throwing up for most of the trip because I'd been bitten by a white tip spider and the bite had become infected. I had to go on antibiotics, which worked against my seasickness tablets and made me twice as sick as I get normally. It was a rough trip but the fishing was insane, plus Paul was really easy to be around and a very funny bloke.

Adri and I have become good friends with Paul and his wife Cristy. They came over to Valencia for my final MotoGP race. Now I've retired I'd like to film more fishing shows with him and learn as much as I can about all the different kinds of fishing around Australia. The thing I like most about the sport is the unpredictability. Some days you can fish all day and not catch a single thing and you'll be scratching your head wondering why and then the next day you can't keep them off your line. Again it's a sport that appeals to my competitive side, of constantly wanting to improve, and I know fishing is something I will be able to enjoy for the rest of my life.

I certainly don't plan to return to motorcycle racing at this point but I'd still really like to help find some fresh Australian talent if I can. I might turn up at a few dirt-track meetings and have a look if there are any quick kids out there but believe me, more than looking for natural talent I'll be looking for attitude, because without it they are going nowhere, with or without support.

We have a couple of kids showing promise in the World Championship at the moment but for some reason they seem to be challenging for the podium one weekend and struggling for points the next. How do you explain that? It has to be a motivational thing. People complain about a lack of opportunities out there but that's never been any different. Teams survive on riders bringing in money but they still have to get results and if somebody special comes along they'll find a space for them. I'd be happy to help if I find the right kid. I don't think we could ever have achieved what we did if it wasn't for people extending a hand here or there; guys like Terry Pav, Ian Newton, Paul Feeney, George Lloyd, Alberto Puig, Lucio Cecchinello and James Strong.

Looking back at the end of my motorcycling career I feel a mixture of emotions. I won two World Championships, travelled the world, met great people and because of motor racing met my wife. I have a beautiful home, my health, a precious daughter, a great family and I don't have to work again if I don't want to. What more can I ask for than that?

I know I said earlier I don't believe in luck and it's true, I have worked hard to get to this point but I can still say I am a very lucky man. I hope that in sharing my story I might inspire others to follow their dream and push the limits of what they can do. If I had any advice to pass on it is to trust your instincts, do it your way and never, ever, ever give up.

Who knows where you may end up!

CASEY STONER
STATISTICS

DATE	GRAND PRIX	RESULT	MILESTONE
July 2001	Great Britain/ Donington/125cc	17	Grand Prix debut as a wildcard rider at the age of fifteen
October 2001	Australia/Phillip Island/125cc	12	Finishes in the points in second GP appearance and the first at home Grand Prix
May 2002	Spain/Jerez/250cc	6	Finishes sixth in third start as a full-time Grand Prix rider in the 250cc class – the youngest-ever rider to finish in the top six in the intermediate class of GP racing
July 2003	Germany/ Sachsenring/125cc	2	Second place finish at Germany GP – making Casey the youngest Australian rider to finish on a GP podium. Held this record until Arthur Sissis finished third in the Moto3 race at Phillip Island in 2012
November 2003	Valencia/Ricardo Tormo/125cc	1	Becomes the youngest-ever Australian to take a Grand Prix win

DATE	GRAND PRIX	RESULT	MILESTONE
October 2004	Malaysia/ Sepang/125cc	1	Gives the KTM factory their first-ever Grand Prix victory
April 2005	Portugal/ Estoril/250cc	1	Wins on second race back in the 250cc class – the youngest-ever Australian to win an intermediate-class Grand Prix race
October 2005	Turkey/ Istanbul/250cc	1	Wins for the fifth time in 2005 and finishes in second place in the final championship classification
March 2006	Spain/Jerez/ MotoGP	6	Finishes sixth in debut race on a MotoGP machine, riding a Honda for the LCR team
April 2006	Qatar/Losail/ MotoGP	5	Qualifies on pole in second start in MotoGP to become the second youngest rider of all time to start from pole in the premier class; the only rider to start from pole at a younger age was Freddie Spencer
April 2006	Turkey/Istanbul/ MotoGP	2	Finishes on the podium in third MotoGP start – the youngest Australian rider to finish on the podium in the premier class
March 2007	Qatar/Losail/ MotoGP	1	Wins in first race for Ducati – the youngest Australian to win in the premier-class and also the first Australian rider to win in 125cc, 250cc and MotoGP/500cc
June 2007	Italy/Mugello/ MotoGP	4	Starts from pole for the first time since joining the Ducati factory team
June 2007	Catalan/Barcelona/ MotoGP	1	With this win in Catalunya becomes the first rider to win four times in one season on a Ducati

DATE	GRAND PRIX	RESULT	MILESTONE
July 2007	USA/Laguna Seca/ MotoGP	1	Wins from pole and topped all four practice sessions to become the first non-American rider to win at Laguna Seca in the MotoGP era
September 2007	San Marino/ Misano/MotoGP	1	Wins three successive races for the first time and is the first to do so on a European manufactured bike since Giacomo Agostini in 1972
September 2007	Japan/Motegi/ MotoGP	6	Becomes the youngest rider to win the premier-class world title since Freddie Spencer in 1983 and the first to win the title on a Ducati
October 2007	Australia/Phillip Island/MotoGP	1	Wins at home in Australia for the first time
November 2007	Malaysia/Sepang/ MotoGP	1	Takes tenth win of the year
March 2008	Qatar/Losail/ MotoGP	1	Wins the first-ever MotoGP race to take place at night under floodlights
August 2008	Czech/Brno/ MotoGP	DNF	Crashes out of the race on the seventh lap while leading – his first non-finish on a Ducati
August 2008	San Marino/ Misano/MotoGP	DNF	Qualifies on pole for the seventh successive race – the longest sequence of successive poles in the MotoGP era
April 2009	Qatar/Losail/ MotoGP	1	Wins the opening race of the year for the third successive season
May 2009	Italy/Mugello/ MotoGP	1	Gives Ducati their first-ever premier-class win at the Italian Grand Prix

CASEY STONER

DATE	GRAND PRIX	RESULT	MILESTONE
September 2010	Aragon/MotoGP	1	Wins the first MotoGP race to be held at the new Aragon circuit
October 2010	Australia/Phillip Island/MotoGP	1	Wins home GP at Phillip Island for the fourth successive year. This was Casey's last win on a Ducati
November 2010	Valencia/Ricardo Tormo/MotoGP	2	Qualifies on pole and finishes second in his last race for Ducati
March 2011	Qatar/Losail/ MotoGP	1	Qualifies on pole and wins first race with the Repsol Honda team
April 2011	Spain/Jerez/ MotoGP	DNF	Is taken out of the race by Rossi – his only non-podium finish in 2011
June 2011	Great Britain/ Silverstone/MotoGP	1	With this win at Silverstone, becomes the first Honda rider to win three successive MotoGP races since Rossi in 2003. This win gives Casey the lead in the World Championship classification
July 2011	USA/Laguna Seca/ MotoGP	1	Wins for the fifth time in 2011 – the highest number of wins by a Honda rider during the 800cc era of MotoGP
October 2011	Japan/Motegi/ MotoGP	3	Starts on pole for the tenth time in 2011 – a new record for most pole positions in a season during the MotoGP era
October 2011	Australia/Phillip Island/MotoGP	1	Qualifies on pole for the eleventh time in 2011, wins his home race for the fifth successive year and clinches second MotoGP World Championship title
November 2011	Valencia/Ricardo Tormo/MotoGP	1	Wins after qualifying on pole for the twelfth time in 2011 to equal the record for most pole positions in the premier class in a single season, set by Mick Doohan in 1997

DATE	GRAND PRIX	RESULT	MILESTONE
May 2012	Portugal/Estoril/MotoGP	1	Wins for the first time at Estoril, which resulted in Casey having won at every track on which he competed in the MotoGP class
June 2012	Catalunya/MotoGP	4	This fourth place finish at the Catalan Grand Prix ended a sequence of nineteen successive podium finishes
October 2012	Australia/Phillip Island/MotoGP	1	Wins home Grand Prix for the sixth successive year, after becoming the first rider in the MotoGP era to qualify on pole at a circuit for five successive years

Official statistics compiled by Dr Martin Raines

ACKNOWLEDGEMENTS

Over the years so many people have helped me during my career that it is impossible to try and thank them all without missing someone important.

I am not going to take that risk. I am sure they realise how much I have appreciated their assistance.

However, there are some people who have helped me put this book together and I would like to acknowledge them here.

Matthew Roberts talked to many people to fill in the moments I may have forgotten. Mum and Dad and Adri read these pages probably more times than they'd have liked to help me get things right.

Rhys Edwards also gave advice and read through the pages. Jeanne-Claude Strong wrote a beautiful foreword. I'd also like to thank my sister, Kelly, and Adri's family.

Thanks also to everyone who made time to talk to Matt or took the time to make comments that have been included in the book. People like Terry Paviell, Paul Feeney, Lyle Hellyer, Ian Newton, Chaz Davies, Mario Rubatto, Cristian Gabbarini, Anthony Peden, Livio Suppo, Filippo Preziosi, Dr Neil Halpin, and Shuhei Nakamoto.

Thanks also to Hachette Australia, Orion UK and The Australian Grand Prix Corporation for supporting the book.

And, finally, to everyone who gets to this page in the story. I hope you enjoyed the read.

INDEX